Selected Papers from the Asia-Pacific Conference on Economics & Finance (APEF 2016)

Evan Lau · Lee-Ming Tan
Jing Hee Tan
Editors

Selected Papers from the Asia-Pacific Conference on Economics & Finance (APEF 2016)

Springer

Editors
Evan Lau
Faculty of Economics and Business
Universiti Malaysia Sarawak
Kota Samarahan, Sarawak
Malaysia

Jing Hee Tan
East Asia Institute of Management
Singapore
Singapore

Lee-Ming Tan
East Asia Research Pte. Ltd
Singapore
Singapore

ISBN 978-981-10-3565-4 ISBN 978-981-10-3566-1 (eBook)
DOI 10.1007/978-981-10-3566-1

Library of Congress Control Number: 2017931343

Printed on acid-free paper

This Springer imprint is published by Springer Nature
The registered company is Springer Nature Singapore Pte Ltd.
The registered company address is: 152 Beach Road, #21-01/04 Gateway East, Singapore 189721, Singapore

Preface

The 2016 Asia-Pacific Conference on Economics & Finance (APEF 2016), jointly organized by East Asia Research and East Asia Institute of Management and supported by BEFfore from Universiti Malaysia Sarawak, was held on the 27th and 28th July 2016 in Singapore at the EASB campus.

The special theme for APEF 2016 was "Will the current oil crisis and China market slowdown result in a global recession more brutal than 2008? What are the current top global economic challenges?"

APEF 2016 achieved the objective of bringing together leading scholars, students, and practitioners from overseas to Singapore for an academic exchange. The programme consisted of an opening speech by Dr. Andrew Chua, Principal of East Asia Institute of Management, and two plenary lectures by Dr. Evan Lau, Associate Professor, Director of Centre for Business Economics and Finance Forecasting (BEFfore), UNIMAS, and Dr. HUSZAR, Zsuzsa Reka, Department of Finance at National University of Singapore (NUS) Business School.

A total of 60 registered delegates from the following countries attended APEF 2016: Australia, Bangladesh, Canada, China, Columbia, Egypt, France, India, Indonesia, Israel, Japan, South Korea, Latvia, Malaysia, Russian Federation, Slovak Republic, Sri Lanka, Singapore, Taiwan, Thailand, UK, and USA. Participants were invited to submit papers to the present volume. We thank APEF 2016 conference chair Dr. Evan Lau, Associate Professor, Director of Centre for Business Economics and Finance Forecasting (BEFfore), UNIMAS, for coordinating the review of the submitted papers.

East Asia Research (EAR)

Established in Singapore in 2015, East Asia Research (EAR) envisions being the gateway to improving lives and enhancing productivity in Asia through promoting the cross-geographical exchange of ideas and knowledge in various faculties. This will be achieved through the dissemination of knowledge from the Asia-focused research conferences and publications by EAR.

EAR academic conferences provide a meaningful platform for researchers, postgraduates, academicians, and industry practitioners to share unique insights and drive innovation. This is a great opportunity for expanding contact networks beyond a singular field and kick-starting a strategic collaboration. Such partnership can bridge the resources and expertise of multiple disciplines to spearhead pioneer movements, thus giving rise to breakthroughs in long-standing issues.

Kota Samarahan, Malaysia — Evan Lau
Singapore — Lee-Ming Tan
Singapore — Jing Hee Tan

Acknowledgements

This book is dedicated to the memory of my beloved mother, Mdm Pang Soon Kwee, 冯春桂 (1944–2016). You will always live on in our hearts—Lee-Ming Tan, 陈礼铭.

APEF Advisory Board

Conference Chair

Committee Members

Conference Organiser

East Asia Research

EASB
East Asia Institute of Management

Conference Sponsors

Qatar Airways

Routledge Taylor and Francis Group

Contents

About the Editors

Dr. Evan Lau is a well-trained University Putra Malaysia graduate with vast experience and research excellence covering the areas of International Economics with numerous applications of econometrics techniques. Recently he ventured into socioeconomic discipline including Economics of Crime and Suicide. He joined Faculty of Economics and Business University Malaysia Sarawak (UNIMAS) in 2005 soon after completing his Ph.D. in 2004. He has served as Associate Professor since June 2014 and is the current Managing Editor of International Journal of Business and Society (IJBS), an internationally refereed journal indexed in the SCOPUS bibliographic database, Emerging Sources of Citation Index (ESCI), Malaysian Citation Centre (MCC), ProQuest publisher, Ulrich's Periodicals Directory, Cabell's Directories (Economics, Finance and Management), and EBSCO Host Publishing. He is the director of Centre of Excellence for Business, Economics and Finance Forecasting (BEFfore) as well as UNIMAS, which—among other—serves as a platform and reference point for business, economic, and finance forecasting. He was the Visiting Scholar in Faculty of Economics at the University of Cambridge from October 2013 to April 2014.

Mr. Lee-Ming Tan is the founder of East Asia Research, and he obtained his Masters Degree in Applied Finance from the University of Adelaide. He is deeply interested in how humans function and react with each other. Insight into how people's minds work and how they people together is invaluable in just about every field. Outside of work, he enjoys outdoor activities and occasional computer games.

Dr. Jing Hee Tan is an Executive Director of East Asia Institute of Management as well as the Chairman of its Academic Board. He has worked as a Retail Manager, a Senior Science Master of a government secondary school, and as a Merchandising Manager of Robinsons Departmental Store with responsibilities in its Menswear Division. In 1973, he joined the Singapore Institute of Management and eventually became its Chief Operating Officer. In 1994, he wrote his doctoral thesis on Developing a Factor Model of Management Work in Singapore, for which he was awarded his Ph.D. from Henley Management College/Brunel University.

Evaluation of Cluster-Development Strategic Outlooks Using Book Value and Revenue Multiples

Egor Koshelev, Sergey Yashin and Nadezhda Yashina

Abstract This paper suggests an approach making it possible to recognize a core company of a future innovative and industrial cluster in order to subsequently expand this type of business up to a pilot cluster of the region. For that end, it is proposed to use book value multiples, Tobin's Q multiple, and revenue multiples, which allow to determine whether the company in question will be able to become a core of a potential cluster in the very near future. The multiples can also help verify whether a large company meets its current position of the "cluster core." With this end in view, the company's book value multiple is compared with the profitability spread, and the revenue multiples are compared with the profit margin. If the values of the multiples are low, and the profitability spread and the profit margin are high, and if Tobin's Q multiple is >1, the company is underestimated in the stock market and will be developing in years to come more rapidly than other companies in the industry or cluster.

Keywords Cluster · Cluster core · Book value multiple · Revenue multiple · Brand value

E. Koshelev (✉) · S. Yashin
Department of Management and Public Administration, Lobachevsky University,
23 Prospekt Gagarina, 603950 Nizhni Novgorod, Russia
e-mail: ekoshelev@yandex.ru

S. Yashin
e-mail: jashinsn@yandex.ru

N. Yashina
Department of Finance and Credit, Lobachevsky University,
23 Prospekt Gagarina, 603950 Nizhni Novgorod, Russia
e-mail: yashina@iee.unn.ru

E. Lau et al. (eds.), *Selected Papers from the Asia-Pacific Conference on Economics & Finance (APEF 2016)*, DOI 10.1007/978-981-10-3566-1_1

1 Introduction

In the context of economic globalization, present-day globally accepted methods for economic management of countries and their regions become increasingly relevant. Russia's continuing integration into the world economy charges both the government and companies with new tasks, which are aimed to improve the country's compliance with the world's advanced technologies including management of the economy and finance. For instance, applying IFRS standards in financial statements of public companies has become a prerequisite of their recognition in the market as well as their future development.

Clusters are also of paramount importance in such globalization process (Porter 1998; Tukkel et al. 2013). Despite their great variety in the economy, this article emphasizes regional innovational and industrial clusters. Such variety of rules and methods of economic management by regional companies and, most importantly, a variety of methods of interaction between companies result in the formation and successful development of informal groups of companies. Such companies may operate in the same industry and in related industries. However, the reality of the twenty-first century is such that clusters indirectly regulated by the government are the most efficient structures in economic and social terms. This makes even stronger the well-known synergistic effect that is common to clusters themselves (Porter 1998; Tukkel et al. 2013).

Although there are a number of standard cluster-management models, which may include, for instance, the following—Leontyev's model (Tukkel et al. 2011; Prosvetov 2012), the matrix approach to cluster management (Bergman and Feser 1999), the gravity models (Bogomolov and Surina 2011), the model of creating an export-oriented regional cluster (Gnevko and Rokhchin 2006; Tukkel et al. 2013), the model of cluster construction based on the fractal theory (Fedorenko 2010), and the processes of cluster formation and evolution—but they have not yet been studied in sufficient detail. The models required for this must adequately describe organizational issues and market mechanisms for their implementation using the relevant mathematical tools for that purpose. Furthermore, one cannot but take into consideration the fact that even in the presence of efficient interaction between three key agent types, i.e., scientists, government officials, and businessmen, it is required to orient a future pilot cluster and its potential further development to brand appreciation of such cluster, which is actually composed of brands of companies constituting its core.

Speaking of an innovational and industrial cluster, it is primarily required to highlight a situation where a potential cluster may start forming around a single core company of the cluster. Such a scenario is only possible if, in the first instance, such company has adequate manufacturing facilities. In any opposite situation, for example, where we consider a tourism cluster, the presence of a single core company will indeed kill the incipient cluster because there will be no internal competition in the region, which might contribute to harmonious development of the area.

Consequently, to recognize a potential cluster in a region, it is required to identify a potential core company of the would-be cluster. Those methods, which we will further

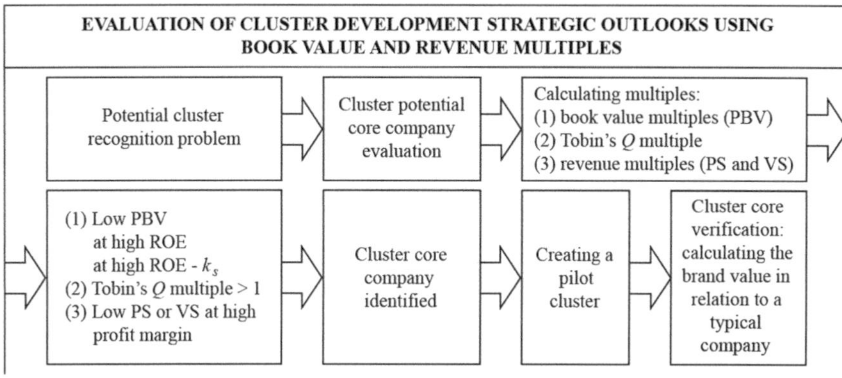

Fig. 1 Concept of evaluating cluster-development strategic outlooks using multiples

present for that purpose, are also applicable for addressing the issue of degeneration of an already-existing cluster in its new manufacturing quality, for instance, from an oil-refining facility into a facility for another type of chemical production or even automobile manufacturing. In such a situation, as always, in operation are market mechanisms that should be simply predicted in due time. Here we mean a situation where any type of business in the market is worth little but, at the same time, has attractive outlooks for further market growth. Such a situation, for instance, in a stock market, portrays itself as a situation of company undervaluation (Damodaran 2002; Roche 2005). Only truly inquisitive financial analysts can detect such trends.

However, in this article we suggest our own approach making it possible to recognize a core company of a future innovational and industrial cluster in order to subsequently expand this type of business up to a pilot cluster of the region (Fig. 1). To that end, it is proposed to use book value multiples (PBV), Tobin's Q multiple, and revenue multiples (PS and VS) (Damodaran 2002; Fernandez 2015b; Pappa 2015; Roche 2005), which allow to determine whether the company in question will be able to become a core of a potential cluster in the very near future. The multiples can also help verify whether a large company meets its current position of the "cluster core." With this end in view, its PBV multiple is compared with the profitability spread, and the PS or VS multiple is compared with the profit margin. If the values of the multiples are low, and the profitability spread and the profit margin are high, and if Tobin's Q multiple is >1, the company is underestimated in the stock market and will be developing in years to come more rapidly than other companies in the industry or cluster.

2 General Description of Multiples Required for Analysis

Currently there are a great number of various financial multiples depending on what exactly an analyst wishes to clarify. However, multiples have the following basic classification (Damodaran 2002):

(1) earnings multiples (PE and PEG);
(2) book value multiples (PBV and Tobin's *Q* multiples);
(3) revenue multiples (PS and VS); and
(4) specific sectoral multiples for IT companies.

We are not going to dwell on all the listed types of multiples. Let us only describe those groups of theirs that will be useful to us in evaluating a potential core company of a cluster.

Thus, constructing the simplest single-phase multiples is based on the well-known Gordon model (Brigham and Gapenski 1993):

$$P_0 = \frac{\mathrm{DPS}_1}{k_s - g}, \tag{1}$$

where

P_0 current fair market value of company share (RUB);
DPS_1 dividend amount on one ordinary share in the next forecast period such as a year after (RUB);
k_s cost of company equity capital (%); and
g growth rate of company earnings and dividends (%)

The Gordon model makes it possible to construct the simplest earnings multiples (PE), book value multiples (PBV), and revenue multiples (PS), which—as do more complicated two-phase multiples when being elementarily decomposed—offer an opportunity to detect changes in basic determinants (constituents) of the multiples and their impact on values of the multiples themselves:

$$\mathrm{PE} = \frac{P_0}{\mathrm{EPS}_0} = \frac{1}{\mathrm{EPS}_0} \cdot \frac{\mathrm{DPS}_1}{k_s - g} = \frac{\mathrm{DPS}_0(1+g)}{\mathrm{EPS}_0(k_s - g)}, \tag{2}$$

$$\mathrm{PBV} = \frac{P_0}{\mathrm{BV}_0} = \frac{\mathrm{EPS}_0}{\mathrm{BV}_0} \cdot \frac{\mathrm{DPS}_0(1+g)}{\mathrm{EPS}_0(k_s - g)} = \mathrm{ROE}\frac{\mathrm{DPS}_0(1+g)}{\mathrm{EPS}_0(k_s - g)}, \tag{3}$$

$$\mathrm{PS} = \frac{P_0}{S_0} = \frac{\mathrm{EPS}_0}{S_0} \cdot \frac{\mathrm{DPS}_0(1+g)}{\mathrm{EPS}_0(k_s - g)}, \tag{4}$$

where

EPS_0 net profit on one ordinary share in the current year (RUB);
BV_0 book value of one ordinary share in the current year (RUB);
ROE return on equity (%);
S_0 revenue per one ordinary share in the current year (RUB);
$\mathrm{DPS}_0/\mathrm{EPS}_0$ payoff ratio (multiple); and
EPS_0/S_0 net profit margin

For more detailed evaluation of reasons leading to certain changes in the values of multiples, they are broken down into even more fundamental variables. The same approach allows predicting the short-term opportunities for growth of the company under review due to current changes in some fundamental variables. Finally, to obtain an even more realistic impression of the current market position and value of the company, a two-phase multiple model, rather than a single-phase one, is used. It implies a rapid growth of the company in the following n years and a stable development in subsequent years. Precisely this method can be used to evaluate, with a reasonable degree of accuracy, future prospects for the development of companies exploring new business lines, the prospects of which are conditioned by competitive advantages of the regions where they are based.

3 PBV Book Value Multiple Two-Phase Model

The price/book value multiple (PBV) may be correlated with fundamental variables. In a particular instance of a two-phase dividend discount model, this correlation can be very easily made explicit. To do this, let us preliminarily introduce the following modifications:

$$\mathrm{DPS}_0 = \mathrm{EPS}_0 \cdot \frac{\mathrm{DPS}_0}{\mathrm{EPS}_0} = \mathrm{BV}_0 \cdot \mathrm{ROE} \cdot \frac{\mathrm{DPS}_0}{\mathrm{EPS}_0}. \tag{5}$$

Then the PBV multiple for a rapid-growing company may be recorded in a two-phase dividend discount model as follows (Damodaran 2002):

$$\begin{aligned} \mathrm{PBV} &= \frac{P_0}{\mathrm{BV}_0} \\ &= \mathrm{ROE}_{\mathrm{hg}} \frac{\mathrm{DPS}_0}{\mathrm{EPS}_0}(1+g)\left(1 - \frac{(1+g)^n}{(1+k_{s,\mathrm{hg}})^n}\right)\frac{1}{k_{s,\mathrm{hg}} - g} \\ &\quad + \mathrm{ROE}_{\mathrm{st}} \frac{\mathrm{DPS}_n}{\mathrm{EPS}_n} \cdot \frac{(1+g)^n(1+g_n)}{(k_{s,\mathrm{st}} - g_n)(1+k_{s,\mathrm{hg}})^n}, \end{aligned} \tag{6}$$

where

- g growth rate of earnings and dividends for the first n years (%);
- $k_{s,\mathrm{hg}}$ cost of equity capital during rapid growth (%);
- g_n growth rate of earnings and dividends at the end of n years continuing infinitely (stable growth rate) (%); and
- $k_{s,\mathrm{st}}$ cost of equity capital during stable growth (%)

However, the equity book value used to calculate this PBV multiple may be negative, whereas the book value of the entire capital is always positive. Therefore, switching to the second case, we do not lose companies from our selection. This brings us to using a two-phase model of the next PBV multiple.

The price/book value of capital multiple (PBV) is a company value multiple. In this case, dividends on ordinary shares (DPS) are replaced with company free cash flow (FCF). Here, a simplified version of free cash flow is used (Damodaran 2002):

$$\mathrm{FCF}_0 = \mathrm{EBIT}_0(1 - T)(1 - \mathrm{RIR}), \tag{7}$$

where EBIT_0 = earnings before interest and taxes (operating earnings) at the beginning of the period of rapid growth or stable phase (RUB); T = income tax rate (%); $\mathrm{RIR} = g/\mathrm{ROC}$ = reinvestment rate; ROC = return on entire capital (%) calculated according to the following formula:

$$\mathrm{ROC} = \frac{\mathrm{EBIT}(1 - T)}{\mathrm{BVC}}, \tag{8}$$

and BVC = book value of company entire capital (RUB).

Then the free cash flow at the beginning of the period of rapid growth or stable phase may be modified as follows:

$$\mathrm{FCF}_0 = \mathrm{BVC}_0 \frac{\mathrm{EBIT}(1 - T)(1 - \mathrm{RIR})}{\mathrm{BVC}_0} = \mathrm{BVC}_0 \cdot \mathrm{ROC}(1 - \mathrm{RIR}). \tag{9}$$

This allows for extending the analysis to cover rapid-growing companies, for which the price/book value of capital multiple is defined by return on capital as well as its value, growth rates, and reinvestments in periods of rapid and stable growth (Damodaran 2002):

$$\begin{aligned} \mathrm{PBV} &= \frac{\mathrm{EV}_0}{\mathrm{BVC}_0} \\ &= \mathrm{ROC}_{\mathrm{hg}}(1 - \mathrm{RIR}_{\mathrm{hg}})(1+g)\left(1 - \frac{(1+g)^n}{(1+k_{c,\mathrm{hg}})^n}\right)\frac{1}{k_{c,\mathrm{hg}} - g} \\ &\quad + \mathrm{ROC}_{\mathrm{st}}(1 - \mathrm{RIR}_{\mathrm{st}})\frac{(1+g)^n(1+g_n)}{(k_{c,\mathrm{st}} - g_n)(1+k_{c,\mathrm{hg}})^n}, \end{aligned} \tag{10}$$

where

EV_0 company market value in the current year (RUB); and
k_c value of company entire capital (%)

The PBV multiple for the whole market is defined by the same variables that define the PBV multiple for an individual company. Therefore, under otherwise equal conditions, the PBV multiple for a market is expected to grow with an increase of profitability spread of the capital (ROE – k_s or ROC – k_c) earned by companies in such a market. To the contrary, the PBV multiple for a market is

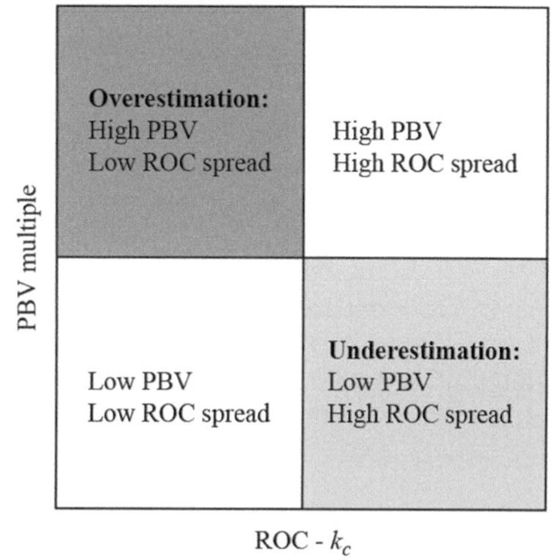

Fig. 2 Price/book value of capital multiples and return on capital

expected to decline with a decrease of profitability spread of the capital earned by companies.

Companies attracting the attention of investors are those in which there is inconsistency between PBV multiples and values of ROE (ROC) or the above-noted spread: low values of PBV and high values of ROE (ROC [or spread]) and high values of PBV and low values of ROE (ROC [or spread]). If the essence of a faulty assessment is associated with identifying companies whose PBV multiples mismatch their capital profitability spread, such mismatch may be adjusted by graphing PBV multiples of companies compared with their return on capital. Such a graph, for instance, for the price/book value of capital multiple is shown in Fig. 2 (Damodaran 2002). Falling within the undervaluation quadrant for the potential core company of the cluster being analyzed, we can maintain that the core company has been found.

4 Tobin's *Q* Multiple

Tobin's *Q* multiple is estimated as a quotient of market value of company assets in place and their cost of replacement (Damodaran 2002):

$$\text{Tobin's } Q \text{ multiple} = \frac{\text{market value of assets in place}}{\text{replacement value of assets in place}}. \tag{11}$$

where inflation increases the cost of replacing assets, or where technologies cut costs for their production, this indicator contributes to a more accurate measurement of asset value than book value. The logical justification of this indicator is simple. Companies earning a negative surplus revenue and not making the best use of their assets will have Tobin's Q multiple <1. Companies using their assets more effectively will be listed at stock exchanges with Tobin's Q multiple >1 (Damodaran 2002).

Although this indicator has some advantages in theory, it has certain problems in practice. The first problem consists in the complexity of estimating the cost of replacement of some assets, particularly if assets are not listed at stock exchanges. The second problem lies in the fact that even when information on the cost of replacement is available, it is required to have much more information to construct this indicator than when handling the conventional price/book value multiple. In practice, to obtain Tobin's Q multiple, analysts often apply time-saving methods using the book value of assets as a reference for the cost of replacement and the market value of debts and equity capital as a reference for the market value of assets (Damodaran 2002):

$$\text{Tobin's } Q \,\text{multiple} = \frac{\mathrm{CS} + \mathrm{PS} + \mathrm{LTL}}{\mathrm{BVC}}, \tag{12}$$

where

CS common shares (RUB);
PS preferred shares (RUB); and
LTL long-term liabilities (RUB)

In such cases, Tobin's Q multiple bears similarity to the price/book value of capital multiple described in the previous paragraph.

5 PS and VS Revenue Multiple Two-Phase Model

The price/sales multiple for a rapid-growing company may be also correlated with fundamental variables. In a particular instance of a two-phase dividend discount model, this correlation can be quite easily made clear. To do this, let us preliminarily introduce the following modifications:

$$\mathrm{DPS}_0 = \mathrm{EPS}_0 \frac{\mathrm{DPS}_0}{\mathrm{EPS}_0} = S_0 \cdot \frac{\mathrm{EPS}_0}{S_0} \cdot \frac{\mathrm{DPS}_0}{\mathrm{EPS}_0}, \tag{13}$$

where

S_0 revenue per one ordinary share in the current year (RUB);
EPS_0/S_0 net profit margin; and
$\mathrm{DPS}_0/\mathrm{EPS}_0$ payoff ratio (multiple)

Then the PS multiple for a rapid-growing company may be recorded in a two-phase dividend discount model as follows (Damodaran 2002):

$$\begin{aligned}\mathrm{PS} &= \frac{P_0}{S_0}\\ &= \left(\frac{\mathrm{EPS}_0}{S_0}\right)_{\mathrm{hg}} \frac{\mathrm{DPS}_0}{\mathrm{EPS}_0}(1+g)\left(1-\frac{(1+g)^n}{(1+k_{s,\mathrm{hg}})^n}\right)\frac{1}{k_{s,\mathrm{hg}}-g}\\ &+\left(\frac{\mathrm{EPS}_0}{S_0}\right)_{\mathrm{st}} \frac{\mathrm{DPS}_n}{\mathrm{EPS}_n}\cdot\frac{(1+g)^n(1+g_n)}{(k_{s,\mathrm{st}}-g_n)(1+k_{s,\mathrm{hg}})^n}.\end{aligned} \tag{14}$$

The price/sales multiple (VS), similar to the price/book value of capital multiple, represents a corporate value multiple. In this case, dividends on ordinary shares (DPS) are also replaced with corporate free cash flows (FCF). Then the free cash flow at the beginning of the period of rapid growth or stable phase may be modified as follows

$$\mathrm{FCF}_0 = \mathrm{EBIT}_0(1-T)(1-\mathrm{RIR}) = \mathrm{NS}_0\frac{\mathrm{EBIT}_0(1-T)}{\mathrm{NS}_0}(1-\mathrm{RIR}), \tag{15}$$

where NS_0 = entire revenue at the beginning of the period of rapid growth or stable phase (RUB); and $\mathrm{EBIT}(1-T)/\mathrm{NS}_0$ = operating profit margin after taxes.

This allows for extending the analysis to cover rapid-growing companies, for which the price/sales multiple is defined by operating profit margin, growth rates, and cost of capital and reinvestments in periods of rapid and stable growth (Damodaran 2002):

$$\begin{aligned}\mathrm{VS} &= \frac{\mathrm{EV}_0}{\mathrm{NS}_0}\\ &= \left(\frac{\mathrm{EBIT}_0(1-T)}{\mathrm{NS}_0}\right)_{\mathrm{hg}}(1-\mathrm{RIR}_{\mathrm{hg}})(1+g)\left(1-\frac{(1+g)^n}{(1+k_{c,\mathrm{hg}})^n}\right)\frac{1}{k_{c,\mathrm{hg}}-g}\\ &+\left(\frac{\mathrm{EBIT}_0(1-T)}{\mathrm{NS}_0}\right)_{\mathrm{st}}(1-\mathrm{RIR}_{st})\frac{(1+g)^n(1+g_n)}{(k_{c,\mathrm{st}}-g_n)(1+k_{c,\mathrm{hg}})^n}.\end{aligned} \tag{16}$$

Although the growth, risk, and cash-flow characteristics have an effect on revenue multiples, their key determinant continues to be a profit margin, i.e., a net profit margin for the PS multiple and an operating profit margin for the VS multiple. Therefore, it is no wonder that we identify companies as having a low profit margin and a low revenue multiple as well as companies having a high profit margin and a high revenue multiple. At the same time, companies with high revenue multiples and low profit margins, along with companies with low revenue multiples and high profit margins, should draw the attention of investors as potentially overestimated or underestimated ones, respectively. Figure 3 presents this in the form of a matrix (Damodaran 2002). Showing companies on it and looking for potential inconsistencies between a profit margin and a revenue multiple, it is possible to identify underestimated or overestimated companies in a sector, industry, or region.

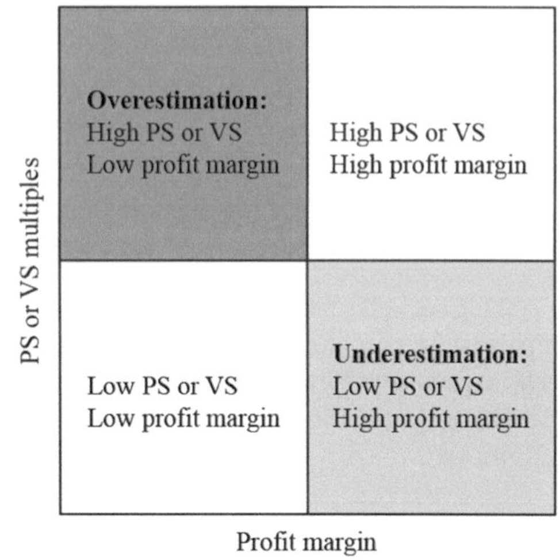

Fig. 3 Revenue multiples and profit margin

This brings us to the idea that it is required to reverify the identified core company of the pilot cluster, for which purpose we suggest further calculation of the core company brand value with reference to a standard (unbranded) company.

6 Cluster-Core Verification: Brand Value Calculation

The standard procedure for adding "brand premiums" to the value of discounted cash flows, which is often established arbitrarily, may lead to erroneous estimates (Damodaran 2002). Instead, the value of a brand may be estimated using an approach that correlates the profit margin to the price/sales multiple.

One of the benefits of having a well-known and respectable brand lies in the fact that companies can set high prices for the same products providing for a higher profit margin and therefore a higher price/sales multiple and greater goodwill. The larger the price premium that a company is able to set, the higher the brand value. In general terms, the value of a brand may be recorded as follows (Damodaran 2002; Fernandez 2015a):

$$B = (\mathrm{VS}_b - \mathrm{VS}_g)\mathrm{NS}_b, \tag{17}$$

where the index b = a branded company, and the index g = a typical company.

It should be also noted that apart from a one-time estimate of the cluster-core company brand value, a positive dynamics of this value is also important.

7 Empirical Results

As an example that we are going to consider in this paragraph, let us take JSC GAZ. This is a company that publishes its IFRS statements, from where one can obtain necessary balance sheet and market data. In addition, GAZ is currently included in the five anchor participants of the Nizhny Novgorod industrial innovation cluster (www.cluster.hse.ru). In this case, it is reasonable to check this company for its compliance with the cluster core. Let us analyze GAZ IFRS statements for 10 years from 2005 to 2014 (www.gazgroup.ru).

The company grows with the anomalous average rate $g = 28.53\%$ throughout the next 6 years and achieves a continuous growth rate $g_6 = 4.09\%$ at the end of that period (Yashin et al. 2015). To calculate the PBV and VS multiples, it is also required to forecast the capital value of the company during the period of its rapid growth ($k_{c,\mathrm{hg}} = 19.37\%$) and in the period of its stable growth ($k_{c,\mathrm{st}} = 16.72\%$) (Yashin et al. 2015).

7.1 *Price/Book Value of Capital Multiple*

In a two-phase model, this multiple is calculated according to the following formula:

$$\begin{aligned}\mathrm{PBV} &= \frac{\mathrm{EV}_0}{\mathrm{BVC}_0}\\ &= \mathrm{ROC}_{\mathrm{hg}}(1-\mathrm{RIR}_{\mathrm{hg}})(1+g)\left(1-\frac{(1+g)^n}{(1+k_{c,\mathrm{hg}})^n}\right)\frac{1}{k_{c,\mathrm{hg}}-g}\\ &\quad+\mathrm{ROC}_{\mathrm{st}}(1-\mathrm{RIR}_{\mathrm{st}})\frac{(1+g)^n(1+g_n)}{(k_{c,\mathrm{st}}-g_n)(1+k_{c,\mathrm{hg}})^n}.\end{aligned} \tag{18}$$

Before calculating its value for GAZ, let us evaluate the company return on equity on the basis of the principle of comparability of the fundamental variable g with its determinants, namely,

$$\text{growth rate} = \text{reinvestment rate} \times \text{return on capital}. \tag{19}$$

It is not allowed to use its actual value in 2014 as $\mathrm{RIR}_{\mathrm{hg}}$ because it is >1 (Table 1). Then let us use the data RIR predictable according to the parabolic curve (Dyakonov 2010; Polovko 2007) (Fig. 4). Eventually, we will obtain that the following:

Table 1 Reinvestment rates, operating profit margins after taxes, and revenue/book value of capital ratio by year

	2005	2006	2007	2008	2009
RIR	0.933302	0.925021	0.936358	1.619123	1
$EBIT(1-T)/NS$	0.071349	0.075426	0.076465	−0.007803	0.092665
NS/BVC	5.967748	4.644949	5.488232	11.812215	−1.356917
	2010	2011	2012	2013	2014
RIR	0.992328	0.999311	0.99531	0.997521	0.999114
$EBIT(1-T)/NS$	0.084199	0.109571	0.076533	0.050252	0.098319
NS/BVC	−4.460571	5.755542	3.552052	5.204766	12.463227

```
data := {{1, 0.933302}, {2, 0.925021}, {3, 0.936358}, {4, 1.619123},
  {5, 1}, {6, 0.992328}, {7, 0.999311}, {8, 0.99531}, {9, 0.997521},
  {10, 0.999114}}
p1[x_] = Fit[data, {1, x}, x]

1.05549 - 0.00286388 x

g1 := Plot[p1[x], {x, 0, 11}]

p2[x_] = Fit[data, {1, x, x^2}, x]

0.862432 + 0.0936654 x - 0.00877539 x^2

g2 := Plot[p2[x], {x, 0, 11}]

p5[x_] = Fit[data, {1, x, x^2, x^3, x^4, x^5}, x]

2.07549 - 2.08542 x + 1.18734 x^2 - 0.270471 x^3 + 0.0266688 x^4 - 0.000951941 x^5

g5 := Plot[p5[x], {x, 0, 11}]
gd := ListPlot[data, PlotStyle → {PointSize[0.02]}]
Show[g1, g2, g5, gd, PlotRange → {0.8, 1.65}]
```

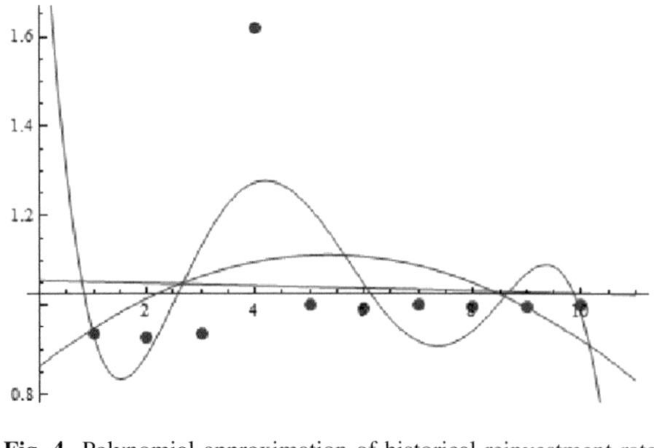

Fig. 4 Polynomial approximation of historical reinvestment rates in *Mathematica* package

$$\mathrm{ROC_{hg}} = \frac{g}{\mathrm{RIR}_{10}} = \frac{0.2853}{0.921547} = 0.309588\,(30.96\%), \tag{20}$$

$$\mathrm{ROC_{st}} = \frac{g_{16}}{\mathrm{RIR}_{16}} = \frac{0.040875}{0.114579} = 0.356741\,(35.67\%). \tag{21}$$

Then it is possible to evaluate the price/book value of capital multiple as follows:

$$\begin{aligned}\mathrm{PBV} &= 0.309588(1-0.921547)1.2853\left(1-\frac{1.2853^6}{1.1937^6}\right)\frac{1}{0.1937-0.2853}\\ &\quad +0.356741(1-0.114579)\frac{1.2853^6\cdot 1.040875}{(0.1672-0.040875)1.1937^6} = 4.245996.\end{aligned} \tag{22}$$

The PBV multiple is high. At the same time, the actual capital profitability spread in 2014 was

$$\mathrm{ROC} - k_c = 122.54 - 19.37\% = 103.17\%, \tag{23}$$

which was a very high value. As mentioned previously, this was due to a high value of the revenue/book value of capital ratio (NS/BVC) in 2014. Then according to Fig. 2 (Sect. 3), it turns out that the company is underestimated (regardless of the high PBV).

Let us verify this statement. To that end, let us first calculate the fair market value of the company in 2014:

$$\mathrm{EV}_0 = \mathrm{PBV}\cdot\mathrm{BVC}_0 = 4.245996\cdot 9{,}627{,}817 = 40{,}879{,}672\,(\text{‘000 RUB}) \tag{24}$$

Then let us compare it with the company actual market value, which in 2014 was equal to

$$\mathrm{CS}+\mathrm{PS}+\mathrm{LTL} = 23,270,333\,\text{‘000 RUB}. \tag{25}$$

Consequently, the company is indeed greatly underestimated in the market.

7.2 Tobin's Q Multiple

We calculate Tobin's Q multiple as follows:

$$\text{Tobin's } Q\,\text{multiple} = \frac{\mathrm{CS}+\mathrm{PS}+\mathrm{LTL}}{\mathrm{BVC}} = \frac{23{,}270{,}333}{9{,}627{,}817} = 2.417 > 1 \tag{26}$$

Tobin's Q multiple is notably >1. This points to the fact that the company uses its assets in an efficient way and earns a considerable positive surplus yield.

7.3 Price/Sales Multiple

In a two-phase model, this multiple is calculated according to the following formula:

$$\begin{aligned} \mathrm{VS} &= \frac{\mathrm{EV}_0}{\mathrm{NS}_0} \\ &= \left(\frac{\mathrm{EBIT}_0(1-T)}{\mathrm{NS}_0}\right)_{\mathrm{hg}} (1-\mathrm{RIR}_{\mathrm{hg}})(1+g)\left(1-\frac{(1+g)^n}{(1+k_{c,\mathrm{hg}})^n}\right)\frac{1}{k_{c,\mathrm{hg}}-g} \\ &\quad + \left(\frac{\mathrm{EBIT}_0(1-T)}{\mathrm{NS}_0}\right)_{\mathrm{st}} (1-\mathrm{RIR}_{\mathrm{st}})\frac{(1+g)^n(1+g_n)}{(k_{c,\mathrm{st}}-g_n)(1+k_{c,\mathrm{hg}})^n} \end{aligned} \tag{27}$$

Because we previously used the average value 0.072698 for the anticipated operating profit margin after taxes, we are going to apply the same method here. Then the price/sales multiple is equal to

$$\begin{aligned} \mathrm{VS} = \underbrace{0.072698}_{\text{high profit margin}} &\left[(1-0.921547)1.2853\left(1-\frac{1.2853^6}{1.1937^6}\right)\frac{1}{0.1937-0.2853}\right. \\ &\left. + (1-0.114579)\frac{1.2853^6\cdot 1.040875}{(0.1672-0.040875)1.1937^6}\right] = \underbrace{0.871171}_{\text{low multiple}}. \end{aligned} \tag{28}$$

According to Fig. 3 (Sect. 5), it turns out that the company is underestimated in the market. Let us verify this statement. For that end, let us first calculate the fair market value of the company in 2014:

$$\mathrm{EV}_0 = \mathrm{VS}\cdot\mathrm{NS}_0 = 0.871171\cdot 119{,}993{,}667 = 104{,}535{,}003\ (\text{‘000 RUB}). \tag{29}$$

Then let us compare it with the company actual market value that in 2014 was equal to

$$\mathrm{CS}+\mathrm{PS}+\mathrm{LTL} = 23{,}270{,}333\ \text{‘000 RUB}. \tag{30}$$

As we can see, the company underestimation in the market is great. Notably, the rating EV_0 based on the VS multiple is essentially higher than that based on the PBV multiple. This is because book value multiples are greatly affected by accounting decisions, which was pointed out in Sect. 5.

However, to identify more thoroughly whether GAZ is actually a core company of the Nizhny Novgorod industrial innovation cluster, let us calculate its brand value in relation to a typical company.

7.4 Cluster-Core Company Brand Value

Let us take two Russian companies operating in the same industry, AvtoVAZ and KAMAZ, as typical companies, with which we will compare GAZ.

7.4.1 Comparing GAZ with AvtoVAZ

Let us use the required information from AvtoVAZ IFRS statements for 2014 (www.lada.ru). Thus, the average book value of capital less current liabilities for this typical company in 2014 was

$$\text{BVC} = 83{,}200{,}000\,\text{‘000}\,\text{RUB}. \tag{31}$$

If GAZ earned the same profit margin as AvtoVAZ and had the same revenue/book value of capital ratio as AvtoVAZ in 2014, then the return on capital and the expected growth rates during GAZ rapid growth would be as follows:

$$\begin{aligned}\text{ROC} &= \frac{\text{EBIT}(1-T)}{\text{NS}}\cdot\frac{\text{NS}}{\text{BVC}}\\ &= \frac{14{,}429{,}000(1-0.2)}{190{,}734{,}000}\cdot\frac{190{,}734{,}000}{83{,}200{,}000}\\ &= 0.06052\cdot 2.292476 = 0.138741,\end{aligned} \tag{32}$$

$$g = \text{RIR}_{10}\cdot\text{ROC} = 0.921547\cdot 0.138741 = 0.127856. \tag{33}$$

Supposing that the profit margin equal to 0.06052 and the revenue/book value of capital ratio equal to 2.292476 will be maintained on and on. In this case, the reinvestment rate required for stable growth will also increase to maintain the growth rates $g_{16} = 0.040875$:

$$\text{RIR}_{16} = \frac{g_{16}}{\text{ROC}} = \frac{0.040875}{0.138741} = 0.294614. \tag{34}$$

With lower growth rates in the period of rapid growth and a higher reinvestment rate, we obtain a far lesser price/sales multiple for GAZ:

$$\begin{aligned}\text{VS}_g = 0.06052\Bigg[&(1-0.921547)1.127856\left(1-\frac{1.127856^6}{1.1937^6}\right)\frac{1}{0.1937-0.127856}\\ &+(1-0.294614)\frac{1.127856^6\cdot 1.040875}{(0.1672-0.040875)1.1937^6}\Bigg] = 0.273723.\end{aligned} \tag{35}$$

The result is that we can find GAZ brand value in relation to this typical company:

$$B = (\mathrm{VS}_b - \mathrm{VS}_g)\mathrm{NS}_b \\ = (0.871171 - 0.273723)119{,}993{,}667 = 71{,}689{,}976\,(\text{`000 RUB}), \tag{36}$$

which is 68.58% of $\mathrm{EV}_b = 104{,}535{,}003$ thousand rubles.

Therefore, 68.58% of GAZ's estimated value equal to 104,535,003 thousand rubles is based on its brand, which provides it with the market power making it possible to earn an excess profit margin and grow more rapidly.

7.4.2 Comparing GAZ with KAMAZ

Let us use the required information from KAMAZ IFRS statements for 2014 (www.kamaz.ru). Thus, the average book value of capital less current liabilities for this typical company in 2014 was

$$\mathrm{BVC} = 54{,}013{,}500\,\text{`000 RUB}. \tag{37}$$

Let us calculate step-by-step the GAZ brand value in relation to this typical company much as we did in relation to AvtoVAZ:

$$\mathrm{ROC} = \frac{\mathrm{EBIT}(1-T)}{\mathrm{NS}} \cdot \frac{\mathrm{NS}}{\mathrm{BVC}} \\ = \frac{6{,}331{,}000(1-0.2)}{110{,}599{,}000} \cdot \frac{110{,}599{,}000}{54{,}013{,}500} = 0.045794 \cdot 2.047618 = 0.093769, \tag{38}$$

$$g = \mathrm{RIR}_{10} \cdot \mathrm{ROC} = 0.921547 \cdot 0.093769 = 0.086413, \tag{39}$$

$$\mathrm{RIR}_{16} = \frac{g_{16}}{\mathrm{ROC}} = \frac{0.040875}{0.093769} = 0.435912, \tag{40}$$

$$\mathrm{VS}_g = 0.045794\left[(1-0.921547)1.086413\left(1-\frac{1.086413^6}{1.1937^6}\right)\frac{1}{0.1937-0.086413} \right. \\ \left. + (1-0.435912)\frac{1.086413^6 \cdot 1.040875}{(0.1672-0.040875)1.1937^6}\right] = 0.13667, \tag{41}$$

$$B = (\mathrm{VS}_b - \mathrm{VS}_g)\mathrm{NS}_b \\ = (0.871171 - 0.13667)119{,}993{,}667 = 88{,}135{,}468\,(\text{`000 RUB}). \tag{42}$$

In this case, the brand value of GAZ is 84.31% of its market value of $\mathrm{EV}_b =$ 104,535,003 thousand rubles.

Now it can be seen that comparing GAZ with the two typical companies operating in the same industry has shown that this company was legitimately selected to be a core of the Nizhny Novgorod industrial innovation cluster.

Moreover, comparing such GAZ brand's ratings of 68.58 and 84.31% of the company estimated value, one concludes that a brand value is not an absolute measure but rather a relative one.

8 Discussion

The principal theoretical result of this article includes the suggested approach making it possible to recognize a core company of a future innovational and industrial cluster in order to subsequently expand this type of business up to a pilot cluster of the region. For that end, it is proposed to use book value multiples (PBV), Tobin's Q multiple, and revenue multiples (PS and VS). They allow to determine whether the company in question will be able to become a core of a potential cluster in the very near future. The multiples can also help verify whether a large company meets its current position of the"cluster core." With this end in view, its PBV multiple is compared with the profitability spread, and the PS or VS multiple is compared with the profit margin. If the values of the multiples are low, and the profitability spread and the profit margin are high, and if Tobin's Q multiple is > 1, the company is underestimated in the stock market and will be developing in years to come more rapidly than other companies in the industry or cluster.

As a result of the conducted empirical analysis, the following practical conclusions have been obtained in this article. Comparison of JSC GAZ with two typical companies operating in the same industry, i.e., JSC AvtoVAZ and PJSC KAMAZ, has shown that this company was legitimately selected to be a core of the Nizhny Novgorod industrial innovation cluster. Moreover, comparing such GAZ brand's ratings of 68.58 and 84.31% of the company estimated value, it may be concluded that a brand value is not an absolute measure but a relative one.

9 Conclusion

Although there are a great number of standard cluster management models, the processes of cluster appearance and evolution have not yet been studied in sufficient detail. The models required for this must adequately describe organizational issues and market mechanisms for their implementation using the relevant mathematical tools for that purpose. Furthermore, one cannot but take into consideration the fact that even in the presence of efficient interaction between three key agent types, i.e., scientists, government officials and businessmen, it is required to orient a future pilot cluster and its potential further development to brand appreciation of such cluster, which is actually composed of brands of companies constituting its core.

To evaluate cluster-development strategic outlooks, we used the multiple technology with a particular focus on book value (PBV) and revenue multiples (PS and VS). They make it possible to accurately identify a company that may become a core of a future potential cluster or check an already existing company for compliance with the cluster core position. The central focus is placed on calculating the brand value of such company because, in our opinion, it is an expensive brand that is capable of creating and maintaining a cluster.

The results attained in the article may be useful to scientists, postgraduates, students, analysts, and businessmen create their own view on managing the processes of creating and developing clusters using, among other things, our model.

Acknowledgements This work was supported by Grant No. 15-02-00102 "Creating a mechanism for managing innovative development of an industrial region (through the example of the Nizhny Novgorod region)" of the Russian Foundation for Humanities.

References

Bergman EM, Feser EJ (1999) Industrial and regional clusters: concepts and comparative applications. Regional Research Institute, West Virginia University, Morganton

Bogomolov VA, Surina AV (2011) Using of model in knowledge distribution assesment. St. Petersburg State Polytech Univ J Comput Sci Telecommun Control Syst 2:195–199

Brigham EF, Gapenski LC (eds) (1993) Intermediate financial management. The Dryden Press, Orlando

Damodaran A (2002) Investment valuation: tools and techniques for determining the value of any asset. Wiley, New York

Dyakonov VP (2010) Mathematica 5/6/7. Complete Guide. DMK Press, Moscow

Fedorenko OS (2010) Stepping up of investment activities on the basis of cluster approach. Econ Syst Manage Electron J 24(4). http://uecs.ru/innovacii-investicii/item/237-2011-03-24-12-20-16

Fernandez P (2015a) Valuation of brands and intellectual capital. Social Science Research Network. http://ssrn.com/abstract=270688

Fernandez P (2015b) Valuation using multiples. How do analysts reach their conclusions. Social Science Research Network. http://ssrn.com/abstract=274972

Gnevko VA, Rokhchin VE (2006) Issues of theory and practice of regional strategic management. Spat Econ 4:101–114

Pappa AA (2015) Valuation study of Hellenic Telecommunications Organisation S. A. Int J Bus Innovation Res 9(2):188–209

Polovko AM (2007) Mathematica for students. BHV-Petersburg, St. Petersburg

Porter ME (1998) On competition. Harvard Business School Press, Boston

Prosvetov GI (2012) Mathematical methods and models in economy: problems and solutions: teaching and practical aid. Alpha-Press, Moscow

Roche J (2005) The value of nothing: mastering business valuations. LES50NS (PUBLISHING) Limited, London

Tukkel IL, Surina AV, Kultin NB (2011) Management of innovation projects: textbook. BHV-Petersburg, St. Petersburg

Tukkel IL, Golubev SA, Surina AV, Tsvetkova NA (2013) Methods and tools for managing innovative development of industrial facilities. BHV-Petersburg, St. Petersburg

Yashin SN, Trifonov Yu V, Koshelev EV (2015) Evaluation of the strategic prospects for the development of clusters using the book value and sales multiples. Innovations 11:35–49

Disposition Effect on Investment Decision Making: Explanation of Regulatory-Focus Theory

I Made Surya Negara Sudirman, Andry Irwanto and Basuki

Abstract The disposition effect is the tendency of investors to sell stocks early when the price increases and hold stocks longer when this price decreases. As a consequence, investors may lose opportunities to gain greater profits from a stock winner whose price continues to rise; in contrast, they can suffer greater loss when the stocks continue to decline. The disposition effect is a phenomenon widely studied in behavioral finance. There are two main competing theories attempting to explain this phenomenon: the prospect theory and the regret theory. Although both theories give a fairly comprehensive explanation, they fail to take into account the motivation of investors in making investment decisions. This paper seeks to make a critical review of both of the main theories as well as provide a new explanation related to the motivation of investors from the perspective of the regulatory-focus theory. Regulatory-focus theory explains that individuals can be categorized into two groups, i.e. the prevention group and the promotion group. Regulatory-focus theory adds a more specific explanation that the disposition effect is more likely to occur in the prevention rather than the promotion group. The explanation of the disposition effect based on regulatory-focus -is a novelty in this paper.

Keywords Disposition effect · Regulatory focus theory · Prospect theory · Regret theory

1 Introduction

The disposition effect is the tendency of investors to sell stocks early when the price increases and hold stocks longer when the price decreases (Shefrin and Statman 1985). As a consequence, investors may lose opportunities to gain greater profits

I M.S.N. Sudirman (✉)
Faculty of Economics and Business, Udayana University, Bali, Indonesia
e-mail: madesuryaku@yahoo.com

I M.S.N. Sudirman · A. Irwanto · Basuki
Faculty of Economics and Business, Airlangga University, Surabaya, Indonesia

E. Lau et al. (eds.), *Selected Papers from the Asia-Pacific Conference on Economics & Finance (APEF 2016)*, DOI 10.1007/978-981-10-3566-1_2

from a stock winner whose price continues to rise; in contrast, they can suffer from greater loss when the stocks continue to decline. The disposition effect is a phenomenon that has been extensively studied in behavioral finance since it was revealed by Shefrin and Statman in 1985. In addition, it has been studied and found to occur within individual investor trading patterns (Dhar and Zhu 2006; Leal et al. 2010) as well as aggregate market-trading patterns (Chang 2008; Ferris et al. 1988). It was also found among professional investors (Coval and Shumway 2005; Fu and Wedge 2011; Shapira and Venice 2001) as well as the trade regime and cultures around the world (Barber et al. 2007; Boolell-Gunesh et al. 2012).

Shefrin and Statman (1985) developed a model consisting of four main elements to explain the disposition effect: *prospect theory, mental accounting, seeking pride and avoiding regret, and self-control.* Prospect theory offers an explanation of the disposition effect by assuming that the behavior of selling winner stocks too early and holding loser stocks too long is due to the investor being loss averse. Investors are reluctant to accept the loss of probabilities of a decline in prices that may occur when the stock price moves up, and this is realized by selling winner shares too early. Meanwhile, investors are reluctant to accept the loss of a decline in prices that may occur when the stock price moves down, and this is realized by the investor holding loser stocks too long. Mental accounting briefly describes that decision makers tend to separate different types of investments into multiple accounts and then apply prospect theory in decision-making on each account by ignoring the interactions among accounts. Seeking pride and avoiding regret is a behavior that can be induced by selling winner stocks too early and holding loser stocks too long. Selling loser stocks can induce regret, whereas selling off the winning ones can induce pride. Self-control is a mechanism used to explain the reasons of the investors to realize their losses.

In terms of progress, most researches performed have referred to the explanation of prospect theory (Kahneman and Tversky 1979) to describe the phenomenon of the disposition effect (Barberis and Huang 2001; Henderson 2012; Odean 1998; Weber and Carmerer 1998). Others used regret theory (Loomes and Sugden 1982; Bell 1982) to explain the phenomenon of the disposition effect (Dodonova and Koroshilov 2005; Fogel and Berry 2006; Meurmann and Volkman 2006). The proponents of regret theory assume that prospect theory has a weakness. It does not compare the selected options with the unselected ones in investment decision-making, whereas, in reality, investors always compare the selected options with the unselected ones and use the performance of the market portfolio as a benchmark. Regret theory explains the disposition effect based on the anticipation of regret by investors in the domain of gains realized by selling winner stocks too early, whereas in the loss domain investors hold loser stocks too long.

In addition to criticism from the proponents of regret theory, prospect theory has also been criticized by some researchers finding some results that are inconsistent with the predictions of prospect theory to explain the phenomenon of the disposition effect. Some found that prospect theory cannot explain the disposition effect because the explanation of prospect theory is based on loss aversion, which does not consider the initial investment when investors buy the stocks. If prospect theory predicts that investors are loss averse, it has some consequences on the high equity premium. It leads to some difficulties for investors to determine the choice of investment and also to decide to sell the winner stocks (Barberis and Xiong 2009). The concept of investing happens not only after the decision of share purchase or ex-post but also before the decision of stock purchase or ex-ante. Loss aversion can not be used to explain the decision ex-ante, so prospect theory based on loss aversion can not be used to explain the disposition effect (Hens and Vleck 2011).

As an alternative, regret theory has several advantages over the prospect theory to explain the disposition effect. It assumes that after making a decision under an uncertain condition, investors may regret if the decision is wrong or even right; however, after the emergence of information related to the post-decision, it leads to the selected option being no better than the unselected one. This intuitive assumption implies that the utility function of investors is affected by the realization of the unselected option or of the alternative one. Thus, the investor will always distinguish the selected option from the unselected one and compare the performance of the selected option with that of the unselected one as well as compare the performance of the selected option with that of the market portfolio as the benchmark. Based on these assumptions, investors always anticipate regret in making decisions about the investment. This is realized by selling the winner stocks earlier and holding the loser stocks longer, thus leading to the increased disposition effect (Dodonova and Khoroshilov 2005; Fogel and Berry 2006; Muermann and Volkman 2006).

Although the proponents of regret theory states that it has more advantages than the prospect theory, in reality both of them have some limitations in explaining the phenomenon of the disposition effect. Regret theory assumes that every investor always compares the selected option with the unselected one and compare the performance of the selected option to that of the market portfolio as the benchmark. It considers that all investors are very fragile in their utility function depending on the performance of the selected option and that of the market portfolio as the benchmark. In fact, investors have some motivation to make their utility function not as fragile as it is predicted by regret theory. Furthermore, the motivation of every investor has some implications in the ways used to achieve the objectives (Idson et al. 2000). In making decision about investment, investors are always going through a process of self-regulation (Zhou and Pham 2004). This is the process in which a person defines the objectives to choose the means to achieve the goal and to assess the progress of the achievements (Carver and Scheier 1998).

The limitations of Prospect Theory to explain the disposition effect are thoroughly described as follows: First, it does not take into account the selected and unselected options when making investment decisions. In fact, investors always compare the selected option with the unselected one to get the best. Second, it does not take into account the initial investment. The explanation of prospect theory, which is based on loss aversion, has some implications in the high equity premium leading to some difficulties for investors to determine the choice of the initial investment as well as the choice to sell the shares after the decision. It means that the predictions of prospect theory, i.e., that investors tend to sell winner stocks earlier, does not occur. Thus, the disposition effect cannot be explained by prospect theory. Third, it does not explain when or under which conditions investors decide to sell winner shares. Fourth, it does not explain how long investors decide to hold loser stocks. Fifth, it does not take into account the sensitivity of investors regarding gain or loss. In reality each investor has a different regulatory focus with a different sensitivity to gain or loss.

The limitations of Regret Theory in explaining the disposition effect are thoroughly described as follows: First, it does not take into account the various sensitivities of investors regarding gain or loss. In reality, every investor has different regulatory focus that has a different sensitivity toward gain or loss. Second, it does not explain when or how fast investors decide to sell winner shares. Third, it does not explain when or how long investors decide to hold loser stocks.

This paper offers some propositions developed based on regulatory-focus theory to overcome the limitations of prospect theory and regret theory to explain the disposition effect. This paper divided into five sections: introduction, regulatory-focus theory, proposition, discussion, and conclusion.

2 Regulatory-Focus Theory

Regulatory-focus theory states that self-regulation is composed of two different systems: promotion focus and prevention focus (Higgins 1997). Promotion focus is determined by regulatory nurturance needs depending on the approach strategy toward the desired goal, whereas prevention focus is determined by regulatory security needs depending on the strategy of avoiding a series of undesirable conditions. The active-promotion focus under the pursuit of the ideal requirements is defined as the active pursuit of desires, dreams, and aspirations. Meanwhile, the prevention focus, under the active pursuit of what it should be, is defined as active to fulfill responsibilities, obligations and duties (Higgins 1998). The focus of self-regulation of promotion is prepared by considering approaches to the desired state and avoiding incompatibility with the desired state (Florack et al. 2013).

Different tendencies in the strategy of individuals with a promotion focus versus those with prevention focus lie in goals with different destinations based on the individual investor's sensitivity to positive and negative results. Individuals with a promotion focus are more sensitive to positive results compared with those having a prevention focus. Meanwhile, individuals with a prevention focus are more sensitive to negative outcomes compared with those having a promotion focus (Florack et al. 2013). The sensitivity of the individual regarding positive and negative results determines the choice of strategies in achieving the desired goals. In the context of investment, individuals with a promotion focus are more sensitive on positive results, which causes them to hold stocks with superior performance longer and sell stocks with inferior performance earlier. Individuals with a prevention focus do the opposite: They sell stocks with superior performance earlier and hold stocks with inferior performance longer (Kim and Ha 2016).

If investors act in accordance with the sensitivity of the results, investors with a promotion focus will take some actions based on their sensitivity to positive results, whereas those with a prevention focus will act in accordance with their sensitivity to the negative result. Thus, they act in accordance with the regulatory fit. The individual investors acting in accordance with regulatory fit tend to have lower regret intensity compared with those who do not act in accordance with regulatory fit. The ones acting in accordance with regulatory fit feel continuously involved in sustainable activities and have an orientation and interest in the decisions made (Higgins 2000a). Regulatory fit makes people feel stronger and justified in what they have already done so that they are able to pursue the same goals with different orientations and in different ways (Higgins 2000b). Regulatory fit affects the strength of the value of the experience and the feelings of success, which is independent from pain and/or pleasure felt toward the results (Frietas and Higgins 2002).

Individuals with a promotion focus are more prone to accept a new investment choice and take risks, and they tend to rely on emotion and bias in making investment decisions. In contrast, individuals with a prevention focus prefer to hang on to old investments or maintain the status quo, are more conservative in selecting investments, and indicate an attitude of manipulative prevention (Kirmani and Zhu 2007). In general, the individual with a promotion focus tries to compete in achieving the goals by taking as many options as possible to reach the objectives. Meanwhile, individuals with a prevention focus concentrate on the avoidance of overlapping goals resulting in careful decisions and a limitation of choices obviously selected (Zhu and Meyer-Levy 2007). Individuals with a promotion focus emphasizes on speed rather than accuracy, whereas those with a prevention focus emphasize on accuracy rather than speed (Pham and Chang 2010).

3 Proposition

Based on regulatory-focus theory, prepositions can be formulated by distinguishing the regulatory focus of investors and entering the rate of gain or loss. Regulatory-focus theory differentiates individuals into two types, namely, those with a promotion focus and those with a prevention focus. Each has a different sensitivity toward positive and negative results. Individuals with a promotion focus are more sensitive to positive results or gain, but those with a prevention focus are more sensitive to negative results or loss. Then, the gain and loss are grouped into two categories to view the sensitivity of each, namely, small-to-large gain and small-to-large loss.

Investors with a promotion focus are sensitive to positive results and will move from the absence of positive results (0) to the presence of positive ones (+1). Thus, it can be understood that the regulatory fit of investors with a promotion focus is in the domain of gain. They will take some actions in accordance with their regulatory fit, demonstrated by taking a risky option to achieve the goal, and obtain a desired, positive result. If the desired, positive results have already been achieved, individuals with a promotion focus will take the conservative option. They become risk seekers when they choose a risky option and become a risk averse when they choose a conservative one. Thus, proposition 1, i.e., that investors with a promotion focus remain in the domain of the gain, is formulated as follows:

Proposition 1a *Investors with a promotion focus will choose a risky option by holding winning stocks longer when the gain obtained is considered still relatively small, thus resulting in a decrease of the disposition effect.*

Proposition 1b *Investors with a promotion focus will select the conservative option by selling winning stocks earlier when the gain obtained is deemed to have been relatively large, thus resulting in an increase of the disposition effect.*

When investors with a promotion focus are in the domain of loss, they will choose the conservative option, sell loser stocks, and then switch to the new option of stock investment allowing them to move from the absence of positive results (0) to the presence of positive ones (+1). Thus, Proposition 2, investors with a promotion focus on the domain of loss, is formulated as follows:

Proposition 2 *Investors of promotion focus will select the conservative option by selling loser stocks earlier without any considerations of small or large loss resulting in a decrease of the disposition effect.*

Investors of prevention focus, who are sensitive to the negative results, will move from the negative results (−1) to the absence of a negative result (0). Thus it can be understood that the regulatory fit of investors of promotion focus is in the domain of loss. Investors of prevention focus will act in accordance with the regulatory fit indicated by taking a risky option to achieve the goal to get the absence of negative results. If the absence of negative outcome is reached, the individual of prevention focus will take the conservative option. They become risk seekers when they take a risky option, and become a risk aversion when they take the conservative one. Thus, Propositions 3a, 3b, investors of promotion focus on the domain of loss, is formulated as follows:

Proposition 3a *Investors of prevention focus will choose a risky option to hold loser stocks longer when the loss suffered is considered still relatively small, so enable them to be back on non-loss state resulting in an increase of the disposition effect.*

Proposition 3b *Investors of prevention focus will select the conservative option by selling loser stocks earlier when the loss obtained is deemed to have been relatively large, so that it is very unlikely to return to the non-loss state, resulting in a decrease of the disposition effect.*

When investors of prevention focus are in the domain of gain, they will choose the conservative option, sell the winner stocks earlier to realize the expected profits without any regard to the amount of profit. Thus, Proposition 4, investors of prevention focus on the domain of gain, is formulated as follows:

Proposition 4 *Investors of prevention focus will select the conservative option by selling winner stocks earlier regardless of whether the gain is small or large, resulting in an increase of the disposition effect.*

Based on the Propositions 1a, 1b, 2, 3a, 3b and 4, it can be understood that investors of prevention focus are more susceptible to the disposition effect than those of promotion focus. In the domain of gain, Proposition 4, investors of prevention focus tend to sell the winner stock faster than those of promotion focus because investors of prevention focus do not pay any attentions to amount the gain obtained. In the domain of loss, Proposition 3a, investors of prevention focus tend to hold the loser stocks longer than those of promotion focus because they pay close attention to the amount the loss and the possibility of returning to the position of non-loss. Thus, Proposition 5, the differences in the susceptibility of investors of prevention focus and of promotion focus towards the disposition effect is formulated as follows:

Proposition 5 *Investors of prevention focus are more prone to the disposition effect than those of promotion focus.*

4 Discussion

Regulatory focus theory is able to explain the disposition effect in a simpler and more concrete manner than the prospect and regret theories are. The weakness of the prospect theory which does not distinguish the selected and unselected options can be overcome with the risky and conservative options under the consideration of the regulatory focus theory. Basically a risky option maintains the selected stock in which the investors choose the tactics of the risk seekers. While the conservative option does not preserve the selected stocks in which the investors choose the risk aversion tactics. Determining a risky and conservative option is based on the comparison of the performance of the selected stocks and of the unselected ones, as well as the performance of the market portfolio as a benchmark.

Principally, every investor must select the stocks likely to generate gains. They have some assessments taking into account the performance of the market portfolio as a benchmark in determining the choice of the initial investment, and the performance of the investment or of the selected option by comparing the target gain achieved to that of the market portfolio as the benchmark. If the target of the gain is reached or the performance of the selected option has outperformed the market portfolio during a certain period of time, the investors will take the conservative option by selling winner shares earlier. The condition is more extreme to occur in the investors of the promotions focus. The investors of prevention focus, however, who are non-loss-oriented, may take the conservative option without considering whether or not the targets have been gained as they are sensitive to the negative results.

If the selected option generates loss, investors with a promotion focus can immediately respond by choosing the conservative option, selling the loser shares and switching to other stocks tat are likely to provide gain because they are gain oriented. Meanwhile, for investors with a prevention focus, it will not be easy to select the conservative option when the selected one produces loss. Investors with a prevention focus will choose a risky option until the loss may still be deemed to be closed by non-loss or break-even states, but the loss is so big that there is no point to turn back to a non-loss state. In contrast, investors with a prevention focus will select the conservative option and sell the loser stock. The explanation of regulatory-focus theory is able to overcome the weakness of regret prospect theories, which do not concretely explain when investors will sell winner or loser shares.

The prospect and regret theories see risk attitude as a constant trait in a particular domain. In the domain of gain, investors are deemed to have the properties of risk seeker. The explanation of prospect theory toward the disposition effect is based on loss aversion, in which investors will always avoid the loss of paper gain by selling superior stocks earlier in the domain of gain. Meanwhile, in the domain of loss, investors will hold inferior stocks longer because they do not want to realize the loss. Selling winner stocks earlier is the nature of risk-averse investors, and holding loser stocks longer is the nature of the risk-seeking investors. Prospect theory does not answer the questions of under which conditions the investors sell winner stocks and how long investors will hold inferior stocks. Shefrin and Statman (1985) tried to answer these problems by incorporating the concept of self-control in the model developed.

In contrast to the prospect theory, the regret theory explains the disposition effect based on the anticipated regret. Investors always anticipate regret in their investment decisions. In the domain of gain, regret will arise if investors lose the gains already achieved in the form of paper gain such that they will anticipate regret by selling winner shares earlier so as to achieve the real profits. However, in the domain of loss, regret will appear if investors realize the paper loss that they suffer from such that they will anticipate regret by holding loser stocks longer so no real loss results in even more regret. Selling winner stocks earlier in the domain of gains shows that the investors are risk averse. Holding loser stocks longer in the domain of loss indicates that the investors are risk seekers. Regret theory does not respond to the questions of under which conditions the investors sell winner stocks and how long they will hold superior stocks.

Regulatory-focus theory sees risk attitude as a tactic in achieving the goals of investors. In the domain of gain, investors with a promotion focus can choose the tactics of risk aversion or risk seeking depending on whether or not the investment objectives have been achieved. They select the risky option or the tactics of the risk seekers when the investment objectives move from a state of non-gain (0) to gain (+1) that has not been reached. If the purpose of investment in investors with a promotion focus has been reached in a state of gain (+1), then they will choose the conservative options or tactics of risk aversion. In the domain of loss, investors with a promotion focus tend to prefer the conservative option or the tactics of the risk aversion because the orientation of the promotion focus cannot be fulfilled in the domain of loss, in which investors with a prevention focus can choose the tactics of risk seekers and risk avoiders depending on whether or not the investment objectives have been achieved Investors with a prevention focus choose a risky option or a tactic of risk seekers when there is a possibility that the investment might move from a state of loss (−1) to a state of non-loss (0). If the investment objectives of investors with a prevention focus have been reached in a state of non-loss (0), then they will choose conservative options or the tactics of risk avoiders. In the domain of gain, investors with a prevention focus tend to choose conservative options or the tactics of risk avoiders because they are non-loss state orientated such that the amount of the gain is not an issue.

5 Conclusion

The disposition effect is the tendency of investors to sell stocks when the price increases and hold stocks longer when prices decrease. There are two main competing theories to explain the phenomenon of the disposition effect, namely, the prospect theory and the regret theory. Although the two theories are good enough to explain the disposition effect, they still have main limitations in that they do not concretely explain the questions of how fast investors sell winner stocks and for how long they hold loser shares. Neither theory take into consideration the various motivations of investors in achieving their investment objectives, thus resulting in various sensitivities of investors in the domains of gain and loss.

To thoroughly respond to the questions that can not be answered by the prospect and regret theories in relation to the disposition effect, this paper proposed five propositions developed based on regulatory-focus theory to answer the questions of how fast investors will sell winner stocks and for how long they will hold loser stocks. Investor with a promotion focus sell winner stocks when the investment objective, which is the gain in the domain of gain, is achieved. They will choose a risky option by holding the winner stocks until they reach the desired gain. If the desired gain is reached, they will choose the conservative option by selling the winner shares. In the domain of loss, investors with a promotion focus will select the conservative option by selling the loser shares earlier because the investment objective cannot be achieved. Investors with a prevention focus will hold loser stocks longer when there is a possibility to achieve the investment objectives. The main investment objective of investors with a prevention focus in the domain of loss is non-loss. Investors with a prevention focus will choose a risky option to hold loser stocks longer when there is a possibility to return to a state of non-loss. If there is no possibility to return to a state of non-loss, investors with a prevention focus select the conservative option by selling loser stocks. In the domain of gain, they will select the conservative option by selling winner stocks earlier, regardless of the amount of the gain already acquired, because the domain of gain is more than enough to make them achieve the investment objective, i.e., a state of non-loss. Changes in the choice of risky and conservative options in the domains of gain and loss occur because the regulatory-focus theory see risk attitude as a tactic in achieving the goal, not as a consistent trait within a domain. Based on these developed propositions, it can be predicted that investors with a prevention focus are more prone to the disposition effect than those with a promotion focus. The explanation of regulatory-focus theory toward the disposition effect is a novelty in the field of behavioral finance.

References

Barber BM, Lee YT, Liu YJ, Odean T (2007) Is the aggregate investor reluctant to realise losses? Evidence from Taiwan. Eur Finan Manage 13(3):423–447
Barberis N, Huang M (2001) Mental accounting, loss aversion, and individual stock returns. J Finan 56(4):1247–1292
Barberis N, Xiong W (2009) What drives the disposition effect? An analysis of a long standing preference based explanation. J Finan 64(2):1–47
Bell DE (1982) Regret in decision making under uncertainty. Oper Res Publ 30(5):961–981
Boolell-Gunesh SS, Broihanne MH, Merli MM (2012) Sophistication of individual investors and disposition effect dynamics. Finance 33:9–37
Carver CS, Scheier MF (1998) On the self-regulation of behavior. Cambridge University Press, New York
Chang CH (2008) The impact of behavioral pitfalls on investors' decisions: the disposition effect in the Taiwanese warrant market. Soc Behav Personal Int J 36(5):617–634
Coval JD, Shumway T (2005) Do behavioral biases affect prices? J Finan 60(1):1–34
Dhar R, Zhu N (2006) Up close and personal: investor sophistication and the disposition effect. Man Sci 52(5):726–740
Dodonova A, Khoroshilov Y (2005) Applications of regret theory to asset pricing. Available SSRN 301383
Ferris SP, Haugen RA, Makhija AK (1988) Predicting contemporary volume with historic volume at differential price levels: evidence supporting the disposition effect. J Finan 43(3):677–697
Florack A, Keller J, Palcu J (2013) Regulatory focus in economic contexts. J Econ Psychol 38:127–137
Fogel SO, Berry T (2006) The disposition effect and individual investor decisions: the roles of regret and counterfactual alternatives. J Behav Financ 7(2):107–116
Freitas AL, Higgins ET (2002) Enjoying goal-directed action: the role of regulatory fit. Psychol Sci 13:1–6
Fu R, Wedge L (2011) Managerial ownership and the disposition effect. J Bank Financ 35:2407–2417
Henderson V (2012) Prospect theory, liquidation, and the disposition effect. Manage Sci 58 (2):445–460
Hens T, Vlcek M (2011) Does prospect theory explain the disposition effect? J Behav Financ 12:141–157
Higgins ET (1997) Beyond pleasure and pain. Am Psychol 52:1280–1300
Higgins ET (1998) Promotion and prevention: regulatory focus as a motivational principle. Adv in Exp Soc Psy 30:1–46
Higgins ET (2000a) Making a good decision: value from fit. Am Psychol 30:1217–1230
Higgins ET (2000b) Making a good decision: value from fit. Am Psychol 55(11):1217–1230
Idson LC, Liberman N, Higgins ET (2000) Distinguishing gains from nonlosses and losses from nongains: a regulatory focus perspective on hedonic intensity. J Exp Soc Psychol 36:252–274
Kahneman D, Tversky A (1979) Prospect theory: an analysis of decision under risk. Econometrica 47:263–292
Kim YD, Ha YW (2016) Who is afraid of disposition of financial assets? The moderating role of regulatory focus in the disposition effect. Mark Lett 27:159–169

Kirmani A, Zhu R (2007) Vigilant against manipulation: the effect of regulatory focus on the use of persuasion knowledge. J Mark Res 44:688–701
Leal CC, Armada MJR, Duque JLC (2010) Are all individual investors equally prone to the disposition effect all the time? Front Financ Econ 7:38–68
Loomes G, Sugden R (1982) Regret theory: an alternative theory of rational choice under uncertainty. Econ J 92(368):805–824
Muermann A, Volkman JM (2006) Regret, pride, and the disposition effect. The Wharton School University Pennsylvania, pp 1–26
Odean T (1998) Are investors reluctant to realize their losses? J Finan 53(5):1775–1798
Pham MT, Chang HH (2010) Regulatory focus, regulatory fit, and the search and consideration of choice alternatives. J Consum Res 37:626–640
Shapira Z, Venezia I (2001) Patterns of behavior of professionally managed and independent investors. J Bank Finan 25:1573–1587
Statman M, Shefrin H (1985) The disposition to sell winners too early and ride losers too long: theory and evidence. J Finan 40(3):777–790
Weber M, Camerer CF (1998) The disposition effect in securities trading: an experimental analysis. J Econ Behav Organ 33:167–184
Zhou R, Pham MT (2004) Promotion and prevention across mental accounts: when financial products dictate consumers' investment goals. J Consum Res 31:125–135
Zhu R, Meyers-Levy J (2007) Exploring the cognitive mechanism that underlies regulatory focus effects. J Consum Res 34:89–96

Author Biographies

I Made Surya Negara Sudirman is a Behavioral Finance researcher pursuing his PhD in Faculty of Economics and Business, Airlangga University, Surabaya, Indonesia. At the moment he is preparing his dissertation related to the phenomenon of *disposition effect*. He is also a lecturer on Finance of Faculty of Economics and Business, Udayana University, Bali, Indonesia.

Dr. Andry Irwanto, MBA, Ak, CA, CMA is a lecturer on Behavioral Finance as well as lecturer on Accounting and Finance in PhD program of Faculty of Economics and Business, Airlangga University, Surabaya, Indonesia.

Drs. Basuki, PhD, M.Com (HONS), Ak, CA, CMA is a lecturer on Accounting and Finance in PhD program of Faculty of Economics and Business, Airlangga University, Surabaya, Indonesia.

Prospects for the Mutual-Fund Industry in India: A Comparative Study with Respect to the US

Iftaqar Ahmad and Jyotsna Sinha

Abstract It has been a difficult time for mutual-fund investors since the beginning of 2016. Retail investors are watching the values of their equity holdings erode. Mutual-fund investors, as well as the fund houses themselves, are dismayed regarding the future scope of investment in the mutual-fund industry. They are suffering from the consequences that occurred when FIIs started pulling money from the Indian share market. However, as investors we should remind ourselves of the old adage "every coin has two sides." The market will revive soon: It is a matter of boom and depression. Sooner or later this phase will be over. In addition, the drawbacks that the financial market brings for us—the mutual-fund industry in India—are growing on yearly basis but not growing that much if we compare it with that of US market where the contribution of US household to the mutual-fund industry is almost 40% (World Bank 2012). The study is descriptive in nature. It is based on secondary data that were collected from books, journals, reports, and Web sites.

Keywords Mutual-fund industry · US · Growth · Prospects

1 Introduction

The Indian mutual-fund industry has gained much exposure and continues to reinvent itself gradually, exhibiting steady growth over the last three decade. Mutual funds need to be pushed. In today's volatile market environment, mutual funds are looked upon as a transparent and low-cost investment vehicle, thus attracting a substantial amount of investor attention. The market participants are in a vigilant mood waiting to see how the industry adapts to these changes. Asset-management companies are restructuring their business models in order to sustain the growth momentum of the industry and provide for increased levels of operating efficiency and investor satisfaction. The industry continues to battle with

I. Ahmad (✉) · J. Sinha
Motilal Nehru National Institute of Technology, Allahabad, India
e-mail: iftaqar.ahmed@gmail.com

E. Lau et al. (eds.), *Selected Papers from the Asia-Pacific Conference on Economics & Finance (APEF 2016)*, DOI 10.1007/978-981-10-3566-1_3

the challenges of increasing investor awareness, low retail participation, high dependence on the corporate sector, and increasing cost of operations. Mutual funds must play an anchor role in directing household savings into capital markets. It plays a very important role in the mobilization of the hard-earned money of investors, thereby boosting the economy by providing finance to the government and large corporations to use these funds effectively and efficiently so that both investors and the economy grows. Investor demand for mutual funds is influenced by a variety of factors.

2 Review of the Literature

Agarwal (2011) pointed out that there has been an incredible growth in the mutual-fund industry in India, thus attracting large investments from domestic and foreign investors. The number of AMCs increased tremendously providing ample of opportunity to investors in the form of safety, hedging, arbitrage, and limited risk with better returns than any other long-term securities. The Investment Company Fact Book (2015) reported that U.S. households rely mainly on equity, bond, and hybrid mutual funds for meeting long-term personal financial goals. In contrast, some investors use money-market funds as cash-management tools because they provide a high degree of liquidity. Investors in developed countries are well aware of the various financial products on the market. They know the attributes and key financial terms of the intangible market. Gupta and Amitabh (2001) examined the growth and development of the mutual-fund industry in India during the period from 1987 to September 1999. The study revealed that the mutual-fund industry witnessed major growth in terms of investible funds, number of mutual-fund schemes, investor base, and range of products offered to investors. Mehru (2004) analyzed the problems of mutual funds in India. There were several problems such as lack of awareness among investors, poor after-sale services, non-disclosure of portfolio by mutual funds, inter-scheme transfer of funds, and lack of professional fund managers. The study points out that mutual funds were wrongly promoted as an alternative to equity investing and created very high expectations in the minds of investors. Viramgami (2009) concluded that income, liquid/MM, and growth schemes showed growth between March 2000 and March 2007. In terms of resources mobilization, liquid/money market, growth, ELSS, and income funds emerged as the most popular schemes among investors, and these three accounted for >70% of the resources. Among various sectors operating in the mutual-fund industry, private-sector mutual funds were the most prominent players. A majority of mutual-fund investors are not clear about the objective and constraints of their investment; in addition, the most important critical gap in this process is the lack of awareness about the existence of risk elements in mutual-fund investment. The new marketing philosophy and strategies place special emphasis on the recognition of customer needs in an effort to provide a high level of quality services (Harrison 2000).

3 Objectives of the Research

1. To assess the latest trends and prospects in the mutual-fund industry in India.
2. To compare the mutual-fund industry in India with the US mutual-fund industry.

4 Research Methodology

The study is descriptive in nature. It is based on secondary data that were collected from books, journals, reports, and Web sites.

Mutual-fund growth from a global perspective: The global mutual-fund industry has boomed during the past two decades. Figure 1 shows a rising trend in the assets of the mutual-fund industry from 1993 to 2013 and it has approximately reached to touch the $30 trillion mark. In the US, mutual funds increased 600% to $14.3 trillion (Global Research Perspective 2014).

Figure 2 shows the worldwide contribution to the mutual-fund industry in percentage form. We can observe that the United States contributes more than half of the total worldwide mutual-fund contribution. Others are way far behind the US in mutual-fund investment.

Mutual-fund growth in India: The mutual-fund industry in India has been continuously growing since its inception in 1964 when the UTI mutual fund was launched. Thereafter, with the entrance of both public and private players, the market was flooded with many innovative financial products in the mutual-fund category. This industry has grown several fold by providing customized products that suit the expectations of investors. In today's global competitive era when trends in the financial sector are changing quickly, it becomes difficult to beat the market and generate better returns. Today, 49 asset-management companies serve the

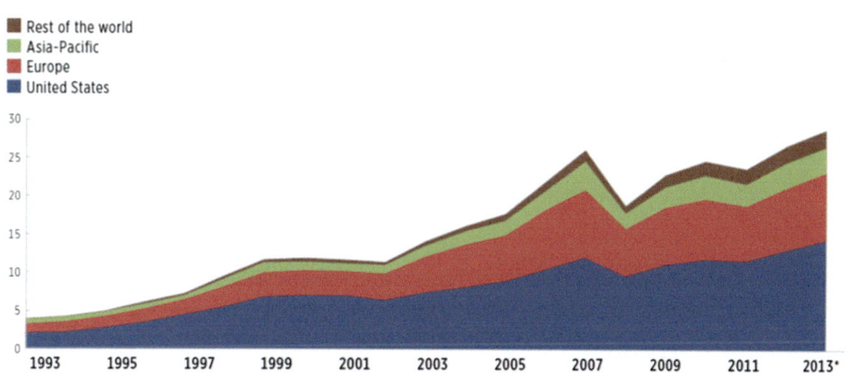

Fig. 1 Growth in global mutual fund assets (trillions of US dollars). *Source* Investment Company Institute

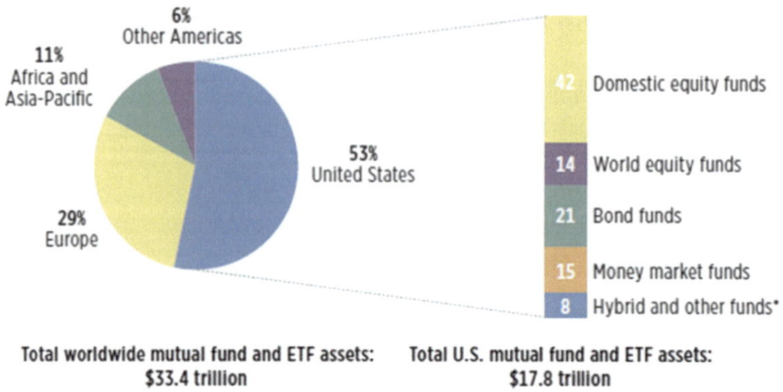

Fig. 2 The United States has the world's largest mutual fund market percentage of total net assets, year-end 2013 *Source* Investment Company Institute and International Investment Funds Associations

Table 1 City-wise AUM of mutual funds in India

City	AUM as of 12/31/14 (crores)	City	AUM as of 12/31/14 2014 (crores)	City	AUM as of 2/31/14 (crores)	City	AUM as of 12/31/14 (crores)
Mumbai	4,08,884	Pune	41,451	Surat	6219	Mumbai	4,08,884
Delhi	1,52,477	Ahmedabad	36,937	Kanpur	5850	Delhi	1,52,477
Bangalore	66,470	Hyderabad	18,092	Panaji	4669	Bangalore	66,470
Chennai	51,801	Jaipur	8018	Lucknow	5479	Chennai	51,801
Kolkata	50,501	Vadodara	7426	Chandigarh	4639	Kolkata	50,501

Source SEBI

Indian public sector, private sector and joint ventures with foreign players. Together the net resources mobilized by them is approximately Rs. 87,942 crores worth of assets (SEBI 2013).

As listed in Table 1, the top eight cities provides almost 80% of the AUM with Mumbai being at the top. This means that mutual-fund penetration in rest of the cities is very low. Many untapped markets remain. India has many opportunities to promote mutual funds in these cities by increasing awareness regarding mutual-fund schemes.

Overview of the mutual-fund industry in the United States: The percentage of U.S. households owning mutual funds grew multifold and has held steady for the past 15 years averaging approximately 45% since 2000.

In mid-2014, 43% of all U.S. households owned mutual funds. The estimated 90 million people who owned mutual funds in mid-2014 belong to all age and income groups, have a variety of financial goals, and buy and sell mutual funds through four

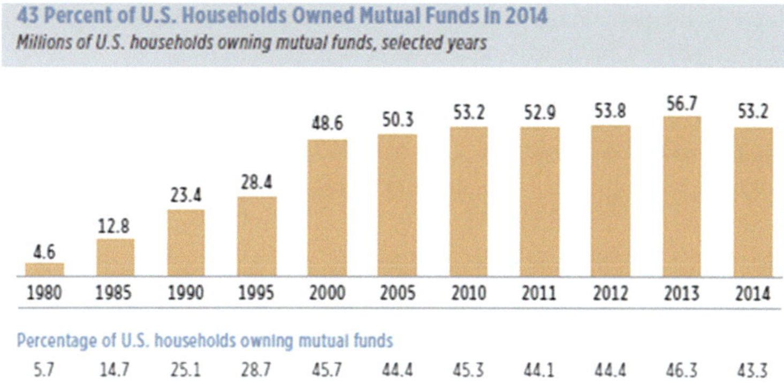

Fig. 3 Percentage of U.S. households owned mutual funds in 2014

principal sources: investment professionals, employer-sponsored retirement plans, fund companies directly, and fund supermarkets. In mid-2014, approximately 90 million individual investors owned mutual funds, and these investors held 89% of total mutual-fund assets directly or through retirement plans. Altogether, 43% of U. S. households—or approximately 53.2 million—owned mutual funds in mid-2014 (Fig. 3). Mutual funds were a major component of many U.S. households' financial holdings in mid-2014.

Findings:

1. Indian mutual funds are one of the fastest growing and competitive segments of the financial sector. The total AUM is Rs. 1,051,343 crores (SEBI 2014).
2. Large parts of the country are not maintaining healthy participation in mutual-fund investment. Only the metro and tier-1 cities have been found to be investing more heavily than the rest of the country.
3. Lack of awareness on the part of investors is one of the single largest factors affecting mutual-fund penetration according to Indian fund houses.
4. The savings propensity of a wealthy district is higher than that of a poor district. The reason behind high mutual-fund penetration could be the presence of agents and distributors.
5. AMCs are of the opinion that investors in metro cities are significantly better informed compared with investors in non-metro cities.
6. Indian investors are investing their hard-earned money in mutual funds mostly at the advice of a reference group or financial advisor. They just want to make money quickly without knowing and understanding the attributes of various fund schemes on the market.
7. The majority of Indian households assume that mutual funds are a risky investment avenue. They are risk averse. In the US, almost half of the population invests in mutual funds.

8. In the US, the percentage of households owning mutual funds is approximately 43%, whereas in India it is only 0.42% at a global level.
9. Distribution channels still seem to play a major role in mutual-fund penetration and service facilitation in India. They do not boost demand for mutual funds through financial literacy.
10. In contrast, investors don not take time to make themselves aware of the various attributes of mutual funds. There exists a complete mismatch between the objectives of the fund and the investors.
11. Mutual funds are basically for retail investors, but in India the majority of investment is made by large NBFCs and corporations.
12. There are so many expenses incurred by AMC of different fund houses, which are still not fully disclosed in percentage terms such as management expenses, etc.
13. Cross-selling of mutual-fund products has been found to be a very attractive option in promoting mutual-fund investing in India.
14. Even today the role of the financial adviser assumes much importance, and the advisor is the touchpoint for the investor. It rests upon the advisor to encourage the investor to purchase mutual-fund products and help achieve his or her financial goals over a fixed period of time.

Suggestions

1. It is important for investors to understand that mutual funds are not just investment products but rather solutions to their financial requirements. The level of awareness of investors' must be increased; otherwise they keep complaining about that they were not told about the negative side of their fund performance. It is of immense importance that the distributor or financial advisor is adequately trained and regulated so that the right mutual-fund product is sold for the right purpose.
2. Proper education should be given in small cities and districts where mutual-fund penetration is very low. An "education on wheels" type of vehicle must be launched so that information is disseminated to the masses. It has become necessary to reach out to people in tier-II and -III cities and educate them regarding mutual-fund investment.
3. Investors are moving out of saturated markets—such as the US, the UK, and Europe—and looking toward emerging markets such as India, China, Brazil, and Turkey to give a new direction to growth. Thus, Indian investors must come forward for healthy participation in order to mobilize their savings for better returns.
4. The distribution of the various fund schemes offered by different companies through the post office will increase the market penetration of mutual funds.

5 Conclusion

The presence of mutual funds in the country is heavily skewed in favor of the top 60 districts of India. Even within the 60 districts, a major share of mutual-fund presence originates from Mumbai. The reason behind this may be due to the fact that Mumbai houses the financial headquarters of most of the large companies, thereby accumulating the bulk of investments through the non-retail or institutional avenues. If the participation of non-retail customers is removed, Mumbai starts looking like the other larger metros of the country. This means that even today retail investors are not so much attracted toward mutual funds. They are heavily investing in other investment avenues such real estate, gold, fixed deposits, etc. Growth in the mutual-fund industry is by and large governed by macroeconomic factors affecting the country such as FIIs draining money from the share market, inflation, the slowdown in economic output, etc. Thereby we see a slowdown in the rate of growth in the mutual-fund industry as well. There is an urgency to fill the communication gaps between investors' and mutual-fund companies through proper channels and government supports mutual-fund growth through digital India.

References

Agrawal D (2011) "Measuring performance of indian mutual funds" Finance India, 2011. Available at SSRN: http://ssrn.com/abstract=1311761

Gupta A. (2001) Mutual fund in India: a study of investment management. Finance India 15 (2):631–637

Harrison T (2000) Financial services marketing. Pearson Education Limited, Essex, England

Investment Company Fact Book (2015) retrieved from website: http://www.icifactbook.org/fb_ch3.html#top

Mehru KD (2004) Problems of mutual funds in India. Finance India XVIII(1):220–224

SEBI (2013) Handbook of statistics in Indian securities Market. Retrieved from http://www.sebi.gov.in/cms/sebi_data/attachdocs/1434443549912.pdf

Viramgami HS (2009) Resource mobilization by Indian mutual fund industry. Indian J Finance III (3), 33–38

World Bank (2012) World development indicators

Social-Marketing Activities to Augment Brands of Faith in Diversified Marketing in India

Perbettan Baba Gnanakumar

Abstract The spiritual foundations in India have entered into retail marketing of Fast Moving Consumer Goods (FMCG). They are competing with multi-brand companies such as Unilever, Colgate Palmolive, Dabur and Glaxosmithkline. In this context, this research sought to determine the following: (1) the social-marketing activities needed for diversity marketing and (2) the basis for segmenting customers in these markets to create "brands of faith." The research was conducted among the customers of Isha products. The research concludes that cause-related marketing strategies are suitable for diversity marketing and that demographic segmentation should be done on the basis of occupation of the customers in emerging markets.

Keywords Brands of faith · Diversified market · Social-marketing deeds

1 The Challenging Factor

Indian retail markets are highly fragmented (Sengupta 2008). These fragmented markets in the retailing sector are dominated by regional unorganised marketers, community-based marketers, cooperative marketers, and diverse marketers. India's diversity marketing involves acknowledging marketing activities toward diversified groups in the form of religion and a regional community-development centre for a social cause. India's diversity markets are influenced by spiritual gurus. The spiritual leaders of Patanjali products, Sri Sri Ayurveda products, Bochanwasi Shri Akshar Purushottam Swaminarayan Sanstha products, Sri Aurobindo Ashram products, and Isha Arogya products are aggressively expanding their existing businesses (Edelweiss Securities Report 2015). Indian diversity markets are no

P. Baba Gnanakumar (✉)
Sri Krishna Arts and Science College, Coimbatore, India
e-mail: gnanakumar12000@yahoo.com

E. Lau et al. (eds.), *Selected Papers from the Asia-Pacific Conference on Economics & Finance (APEF 2016)*, DOI 10.1007/978-981-10-3566-1_4

longer substitute agents but rather change agents in creating brands of faith. Organised retailing units are also selling products manufactured by diverse marketers. Guenther's research contended that the accelerating trends in diversity marketing are the challenging factor for the organised FMCG marketers (Guenther 1992). Due to competition among the manufacturers of diversified groups, spiritual leaders are using societal-marketing deeds to create brands of faith. Establishing a segmentation strategy as well as social-marketing activities currently are the challenging tasks facing diverse marketers (Raghavan 2008).

2 Knowledge Gap

Past research conducted by Hill et al. (2009) and Hittner and Pohle (2008) proved that social-marketing activities in the form of corporate social responsibility (CSR) strengthen brands of faith. Brand loyalty has been built up by CSR programmes (Pivato et al. 2008; Porter and Kramer 2006; Popoli 2011; Hillier's et al. 2005; Majumdar and Patel 2011). However, the trivial relationship between marketing activities, branding, and segmentation have not been considered in past research. The current research aimed to explore brands of faith created by social-marketing activities in a diversity market and to identify the basis of demographic segmentation.

3 Aim and Significance

The primary aim of this research is to identify the social-marketing strategies and segmentation strategies essential for diversity marketing to create "brands of faith." Hence, the study seeks answers to the following research questions:

I. What type of social-marketing activity creates "brands of faith" in diversity marketing?
II. What is the basis of segmenting customers in diversity marketing?

This research enables marketers to determine the integration strategy linking social-marketing activities with brand image in diverse markets.

4 Use of Key Terms for the Research

Diversity marketing is a marketing paradigm that refers to marketing as a way to connect with different individuals in the market who form a homogenous entity (Dahl, Stephan: Diversity Marketing, Thomson 2002). In this research, Isha foundation members are considered as the homogeneous entity.

The term **brands of faith** considers "faith" as a product and attempts to apply the principles of marketing in order to "sell" the product. "Faith" is the customer's attitude toward Isha foundation. The term "brands of faith" has been substituted with the term "brand image" for the purpose of research.

Social-marketing activities considered for the research include cause-related marketing, green marketing, and social-group endorsement. "Social group" refers to the followers of the founder of Isha foundation.

5 The Isha Foundation

The research was carried out among the consumers of Isha products. The consumers of Isha products are the respondents. Isha Foundation is a non-profit spiritual organisation headquartered in Coimbatore in the southern part of India. Isha Foundation products are branded as "Isha" with an image. The foundation markets a variety of 524 products. Isha products are marketed by the Isha Foundation and targeted toward Isha Foundation community members.

Isha Business Private Limited (IBPL) was established by the Isha Foundation to raise the funds needed for social projects. For the purpose of this research, the social-marketing deeds of the IBPL are classified into three segments—such as green initiatives, cause-related activities, and social movements—to promote the common well-being of society. The brand values derived from the green initiatives, cause-related activities, and social movements to the Isha's brands of faith are labelled as "green marketing," "cause-related marketing," and "social-group endorsements".

The green-marketing values of the Isha Foundation are created through projects such as Green Hands, Vanashree Eco Center, and Isha Foods and Spices. The Green Hands project aims to create 10% additional green cover in the state of Tamil Nadu in southern India by planting 114 million trees. The Vanashree Eco Center was established to preserve the ecology and biodiversity of the Velliangiri Mountains in Tamil Nadu, South India. It also aims to educate youth about conservation and ecology through experiential programs. To maintain and broadcast the area's precious environmental resources, the Vanashree Eco Centre conducted crowd tree-planting programs and maintenance campaigns, helped prevent poaching of national wildlife, and worked to safeguard the gene group of this mountain by propagating the inhabitant variety in the region. Isha Foods and Spices products are a nutritious collection of snacks, drinks, Tiffin mixes, and pickles that offer a tempting blend of taste, nutrition, and expediency. The products are organic and made from fresh, high-quality ingredients. The products represent the slogan of Sadhguru—"What kind of food you eat not only decides the physical aspect of your body, it also decides the very way you think and feel".

Cause-related marketing values are created from Isha Craft. Isha Craft markets contemporary home decor, utility, and fashion products. The income generated from Isha Craft is used for mobile health clinics. Isha Craft products depict the slogan: "a labor of love". Rural artisans design the products. The products are made from locally sourced natural materials and are eco-friendly.

Social group–endorsement values of Isha products are created during Isha social-upliftment programs. The Isha projects based on social upliftment include the Action for Rural Rejuvenation, AIDS Awareness Äyush Health, Ïsha-Vidhya, Rural Empowerment, and Gramotvasam programs. All of these programs are endorsed by Sadguru and artists such as Hariprasad Chaurasia, Shiv Kumar Sharma, Dr. Bala Muralikrishna, Sudha Raghunathan, Anuradha Sriram, Usha Uthup, Vani Jayaram, and Manish Vyas. Isha Foundation works actively with world bodies such as the United Nations through its various initiatives and events. Sadhguru often addresses in these endorsement programs the deterioration of human and social values and ecological degradation. Action for Rural Rejuvenation (ARR) is an outreach program whose primary objective is to improve the primary fitness and excellence of life of the rural meager. The project aims to benefit 70 million rural people in 54,000 villages in Tamil Nadu, South India. It will be implemented in two phases over a period of 15 years. AYUSH–Isha Organic Health Systems is a primary healthcare model with an enhanced focus on preventative aspects of medical care. It effectively combines Ayurveda, Siddha, naturopathy, essential allopathic treatments, yogic practices, and physical-fitness programs. Isha Vidhya is committed to raising the level of education and literacy in rural India and helping disadvantaged children realize their full potential. The development seeks to guarantee excellence of schooling for children in agricultural areas to create equal opportunities for all to participate in and benefit from India's economic growth. Isha Vidhya presently operates 9 schools with 5200 students, 50% of whom are on scholarship. The respite of the students pays a nominal fee. Every school will maintain 1100 students. Isha has also adopted 31 government schools in 2012–2013 comprising 26,843 students who will benefit from vital interventions that will impressively improve the excellence of learning in these schools. Isha Foundation organizes Gramotsavam or "rural Olympics." Gramotsavam is not only about sports, but it also provides an occasion to commemorate South India's rural life and civilization. Every year, the event showcases customary rustic cookery and fine arts and crafts and events such as folk singing and dancing. Sadhguru offers the vast community an understanding of communication, a question-and-answer gathering, as well as the unusual prospect of a guided meditation with a Realised Master. Sounds of Isha, Isha Foundation's in-house music band, puts on a merry presentation that culminates in a stunning fireworks show. The yearly episode has hastily turned into one of the most admired events in Tamil Nadu with increasing crowds every year.

6 Methodology

The research was carried out among 1678 customers of Isha products between March 1 and April 1, 2016. The respondents were selected based on "snowball sampling." Of 1678 responses, 1465 were validated after coding. Of these, 1126

Table 1 Data analysis: input-process output table

Stage	Purpose	Input	Process	Output
1	Grouping of brand-image variables to determine impressed customers	Primary data about brand image	Cluster analysis	Five clusters were created
2	Measuring variation between brand image and social-marketing values	Cluster analysis results and social-marketing values	Analysis of variance	There is significant variation
3	Measuring discriminant factors between social-marketing values and demographic variables	Social-marketing values and demographic variables	Discriminant analysis	Income and occupation are the discriminating factors
4	Measuring the association between brand image and demographic variables	Brand image and demographic variables	Chi-square analysis	There is a significant association
5	Integrating social-marketing values, brand image, and demographic variables	Results of the last three stages	Establishing trivial relationship and ROC analysis	Cause-related marketing establishes high brand image, and occupation is the fragmentation factor

responses were found to be reliable. The interview schedule consists of 25 structured questions formulated pertaining to demographic profile, social-responsibility values, and brand images. The perception of customers is measured using a five-point Likert scale. The internal consistency of the responses is measured in terms of Cronbach alpha. The Cronbach alpha associated with the response of 25 questions is 0.72. Social values are classified under the categories green marketing, cause-related marketing, and social-group endorsement. The data analysis is depicted in Table 1.

7 Brand Image

Brand is a sensible impression that creates personal experience and satisfies expectations based on a set of attitudes. Firms initiated brand image in the mindsets of customers by satisfying psychological and social needs. Brand communications reinforce the image through word-of-mouth advertising and by establishing logos/pictures. Through social well-being measures, firms are re-injecting brand-image values. Companies aim to integrate the customer experience with their expectations to create a brand image (Paul 2002).

We use a mechanism to scale down the brand-image values among the respondents. Brand image is measured through the customer-rating method (Driesener and Romaniuk 2006). Cluster analysis is employed to classify the respondents according to their ratings based on brand-image values. Hence, 16 sets of variables that describe the similarity between objects in terms of brand image were selected to formulate clusters. The attitudinal variables were measured on a five-point Likert scale. The attitudinal variables used for measuring the brand image were reverence, honour, down to earth, honesty, daring, charming, spirited, up-to-date, reliable, successful, upper class, cheerful, "outdoorsy," ruggedness, pleasant memories, and stand-by. The number of clusters was created based on the AIC criterion. A cluster centroid was used to differentiate the clusters, and a five-cluster solution was developed.

Cluster 1 had relatively high values on all variables, and it was labelled "impressive." Cluster 2 had second-degree high mean values among all the variables, and it was labelled "stirring." Cluster 3 had third-degree high mean values among all variables, and it was labelled "Striking." Cluster 4 had fourth-degree high values among all the variables, and it was labelled "Modest." Cluster 5 had the least value among the all the variables, and it was labelled "Unimpressive" (Table 2).

The cluster analysis revealed that 56% (both impressive and stirring) of the respondents in the sample were highly conscious toward their brands' image. Based on cluster analysis, we conclude that 672 customers have impressive values toward the brand image of Isha. Hence, these customers are considered to have "brands of faith".

Table 2 Cluster group of respondents

Cluster	Label	No. of respondents	Pie chart
I	Impressive cluster	278	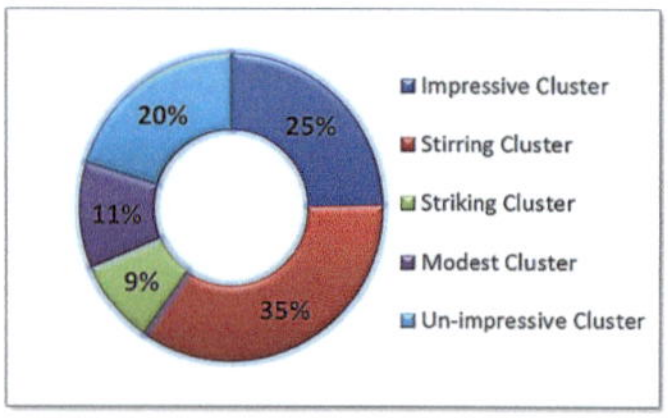
II	Stirring cluster	394	
III	Striking cluster	101	
IV	Modest cluster	125	
V	Unimpressive cluster	228	
	Total	1126	

8 Societal-Marketing Values

Because cause-related marketing, green marketing, and social-endorsement groups are practiced/utilised by the Isha Foundation, we decided to include these social-marketing deeds.

8.1 *Cause-Related Marketing*

We defined cause related marketing as a type of marketing activity involving contributing a part of income to a social cause. Michael's research proved that cause-related marketing activities influence customer choice and create social currency. We employed analysis of variance to determine the relationship between cause-related marketing and brand image. The independent variable is the preference toward cause-related marketing. This was measured on a five-point rating scale. The dependent variable is the centroid variable of the clusters that were created based on brand-image variables. The null hypothesis, i.e., that "there is no variation between the means of the cluster centroid values and preference toward cause-related marketing," was established. The result is interpreted with the associate '*F*' probability value of 0.00 and a level of significance of 0.05. The results are tabulated in Table 3.

The calculated *F* value is greater than the table value. Hence, it can be interpreted that brand image has a significant relationship with cause-related marketing. The relative magnitudes of the means for the five categories indicate that a high level of cause-related marketing efforts leads to create a superior brand image.

Respondents who prefer cause-related marketing were segmented on the basis of age, income, education, and occupation. Stepwise-multiple discriminant functions were formulated to identify the demographic discriminant factor that differentiates the cause-related marketing variables among the demographic factors. Based on the equality of group means, two functions were formulated. The results are displayed in Table 4.

Occupation and income are the two discriminating functions identified by the model. The eigenvalue associated with the first function (occupation) is 0.24. The canonical correlation associated with this function is 0.180. Of the variance in the cause-related marketing variable, 72.2% is explained by this model. The eigenvalue associated with the second function (income) is 0.018. The canonical correlation

Table 3 Cause-related marketing and brand image ANOVA

Variance	Sum of squares	df	Mean square	*F*-value	Significance
Between groups	218.40	4	54.600	24.92	0.00
Within groups	2456.84	1121	2.191		
Total	2675.24				

Table 4 Discriminant analysis of cause-related marketing: tests of equality of group means

Variables	Wilks' lambda	F	Significance
Age	0.846	2.427	0.03
Income	0.923	4.234	0.00
Education	0.912	1.321	0.53
Occupation	0.981	4.980	0.00

associated with this function is 0.086. Of the variance in the cause-related marketing variable, 27.8 percent is explained by this model. The value of Wilks' lambda is 0.946. This transforms to a chi-square of 40.24, with 8 degrees of freedom, which is significant at the 0.05 level. Thus, two functions together significantly discriminate among the demographic variables. However, when the first function is removed, the Wilk's lambda associated with the second function is 0.891, which is not significant at the 0.05 level. Therefore, the second function (income) does not contribute significantly to group differences.

We concluded that cause-related marketing significantly influences brand image. Occupation is the predominant demographic variable that discriminates customers toward cause-related marketing.

8.2 *Green Marketing*

There is a dire need to protect the natural environment. Green marketing was intended to satisfy customers with minimal detrimental effect on the natural environment (Polonsky 1995). Peter Knight's research found that 70% of consumers link marketers' social responsibility to their environmental behaviour (Peter 2008). Green marketing not only involves greening products but also making the organization greener (Aseem 2002).

In diversity marketing, eco-friendly values are created by various forms of projects. Project GreenHands (PGH) is a grassroots ecological initiative established under the aegis of Isha Foundation in 2004. It seeks to restore ecological balance and maintain proper environmental health in Tamil Nadu. PGH was felicitated by the government of India in June 2010 with the Indira Gandhi Paryavaran Puraskar Award.

We wish to determine whether or not there is any significant relationship between green-marketing efforts and brand image. One-way analysis of variance was employed to determine the variation within and between brand-image centroid values of the clusters and preference toward green marketing. The null hypothesis, i.e., that "there is no variation between the means of brand image cluster variables and preference towards green marketing," was established. The result is interpreted with an associate '*F*' probability value of 0.00 and the level of significance of 0.05. The results are tabulated in Table 5.

The calculated a value of *F* less than the critical value of *F* with 4 and 1121 degrees of freedom, resulting in a probability of zero at 95% confidence level.

Table 5 Green marketing versus brand image ANOVA

Variance	Sum of squares	df	Mean square	F	Significance
Between groups	23.524	4	5.881	2.787	0.68
Within groups	2253.411	1121	2.110		
Total	2276.935				

The null hypothesis is accepted. Hence, it may be concluded that brand image does not depend on green marketing.

8.3 *Social-Group Endorsements*

In the diversity marketing system, endorsements are made with the help of regional-level cultural programmes. Isha Gramotsavam is a program organised by the Isha Yoga foundation. Isha Gramotsavam enjoys and encourages the living spirit of the villagers in the Coimbatore region. To promote the program to a great success, >600 teams having >7500 players participated in the events and sports conducted by Isha Gramotsavam. The main events are Khabbadi and Cricket. It is obvious that Khabbadi is one of the traditional games of the South Indians. Some other sports have also been organised including Vazhuku-maram, Uri-Adi, and Silambhattam. Traditional concerts and pageants have also been organised as a part of the program to entertain the audience. The winners of the team will be uplifted and motivated with the Isha Rejuvanation Cup 2015.

One-way analysis of variance was carried out to identify the significant variation among and between brand image and social-endorsement activities. The null hypothesis. i.e., that "there is no variation among the means of brand image cluster variables and preference toward social endorsement," was established. The result is interpreted with the associate '*F*' probability value of 0.00 at the level of significance of 0.05. The results are tabulated in Table 6.

The calculated value of F is greater than the critical value of '*F*' with 4 and 1121 degrees of freedom resulting in a probability of 0.00 at the 95% confidence level. The null hypothesis was rejected. Hence, we conclude that brand image does have significant variation with social-group endorsement. The relative magnitudes of the means of clusters suggest that a there is a linear relationship between social-group endorsement and brand image.

Table 6 Social-group endorsement versus brand image ANOVA

Variance	Sum of squares	df	Mean square	F	Significance
Between groups	32.566	4	8.141	9.444	0.00
Within groups	967.211	1121	0.862		
Total	999.777				

Table 7 Discriminant analysis of social-group endorsements: tests of equality of group means

Variables	Wilks' lambda	*F*	Significance
Age	0.982	7.218	0.00
Income	0.978	0.678	0.21
Education	0.992	1.788	0.13
Occupation	0.872	12.234	0.00

Multiple discriminant analysis was employed to determine the demographic variables that discriminate the social group–endorsement countenances. Two functions (occupation and age) were formulated on the basis of the equality of means. The results are presented in Table 7.

The eigenvalue associated with the first function (occupation) is 0.248. The canonical correlation associated with this function is 0.448. Of the variance in the social group–endorsement variable, 95.4% is explained by this model. The eigenvalue associated with the second function (age) is 0.018. The canonical correlation associated with this function is 0.108, and 4.6% of the variance is explained by this model. The value of Wilks' lambda is 0.724. This transforms to a chi-square value of 3228.612, with 4 degrees of freedom, significant at the 0.05 level. Thus, the functions together significantly discriminate among the social-group variables. However, when the first function is removed, the Wilk's lambda associated with the second function is 0.982, which is not significant at the 0.05 level. Therefore, the second function does not contribute significantly to group differences. Hence, it can be inferred that occupation is the first major demographic variable that discriminates the social group–endorsement variables.

Based on the previous empirical results, we conclude that social group–endorsement activities influence brand image and that occupation is the predominant variable that creates heterogeneity among the social-group endorsements.

9 Associations with Brand Image

The research of Chien-Hsiung identified a positive association between brand image and demographic variables (Chien-Hsiung 2011). Research by Anderson established a social-stratification model that increases brand-building efforts based on socio-psychological variables (Anderson and Cunningham 1972). To construct a relationship among brand image and demographic factors, we employed Chi-square test. The null hypothesis. i.e., that "the brand-image clusters are independent of demographic variables" was established. The results are presented in Table 8 at 95% confidence limits.

The null hypothesis was rejected at a significance level of 0.05 for demographic variables such as age, education, and occupation. Hence, brand image is significantly associated with the age, education, and occupation of the respondents. Because the value of phi, contingency coefficient, and Crammer's '*V*' are <0.5 for

Table 8 Chi-square analysis: brand image

Variables	Chi-square value	Df	Significance	Phi value	Contingency coefficient	Crammer's *V*	Lambda coefficient
Age	84.5	16	Significant	0.21	0.20	0.14	0.08
Income	31.6	16	Insignificant				
Education	78.8	12	Significant	0.32	0.28	0.23	0.12
Occupation	242.6	16	Significant	0.69	0.62	0.60	0.57

the variables age and education, association is not very strong. There is a strong association between brand-image variables and occupation. Hence, stratification can be done based on customer occupation.

10 Diagnostic Test

Cause-related marketing and social- group endorsement activities of firms tend to create a brand image. To determine which of the previously mentioned activities highly influence brand image, ROC analysis was carried out. Realistic-operating characteristic (ROC) curves were drawn to assess brand-image centroid values with social-group endorsement and cause-related marketing variables. ROC curves were used to explore the precision of diagnostic tests as well as determine the best "cut-off" value for impressive and unimpressive cluster test results. The graphical representation of this trade-off is presented in Fig. 1. Setting a low cut-off will yield a very high sensitivity but at the expense of specificity. Setting a high cut-off will yield high specificity at the expense of sensitivity. Table 9 shows the asymptotic significance of ROC analysis.

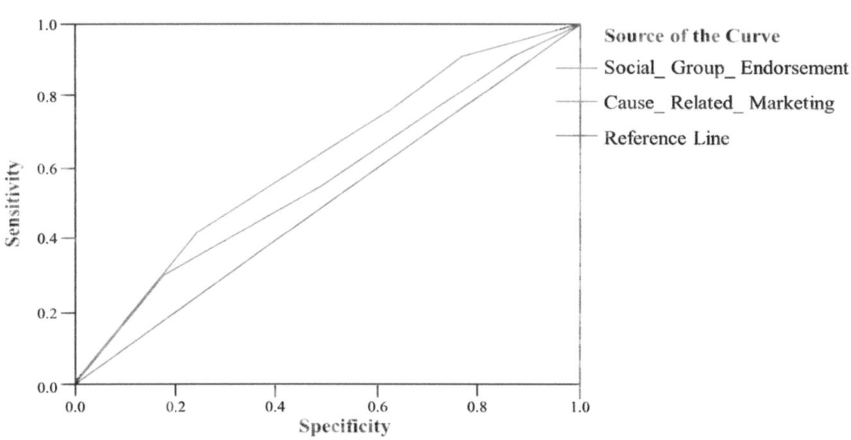

Fig. 1 Brand-image ROC curve

Table 9 Brand-image ROC analysis

Test result variable(s)	Area	SE[a]	Asymptotic significance[b]	Asymptotic 95% confidence interval	
				Lower bound	Upper bound
Social-group endorsement	0.560	0.018	0.001	0.526	0.595
Cause-related marketing	0.612	0.017	0.000	0.578	0.647

The curve of social-group endorsement occupies a minimum level over the cut-off line, whereas cause related-marketing curve overlaps the reference level with a high degree of variation. The cause-related marketing curve occupies a maximum level over the cut-off line. It is also significant at the 95% confidence interval. Hence, it is determined that cause-related marketing techniques can be applied to improve brand image more so than those of social-group endorsements.

11 Establishing a Trivial Relationship

The previous discussions apparently proved that brand of faith depends on cause-related marketing and social group–endorsement activities. Cause-related marketing creates brand image in a leveraged manner compared with social-group endorsements. "Occupation: is the demographic variable that discriminates cause-related marketing. "Occupation" is also associated with brand image. The trivial relationship is shown in Fig. 2.

Hence, we conclude that if societal-marketing activities related to cause-related marketing are stratified based on customer occupation, they will build "brands of faith." Segmentation based on consumer occupation is the foremost discriminant variable. Hence, customer occupation can be used to segment customers as to diverse marketing strategies.

12 Conclusion

Creating brands of faith through societal-marketing activities is a complicated endeavour. Only if the philanthropic values attached to such activities have been recognised by the society as measure of social well-being will spiritual leaders are able to enhance their brands of faith. Social-media communication about cause-related marketing is able to create trust among the society. In contrast, societal-marketing activities cannot target the entire society; hence, they must be stratified. While stratifying, the players of diversity markets must target a particular group based on the values generated by the stakeholders in the foundation.

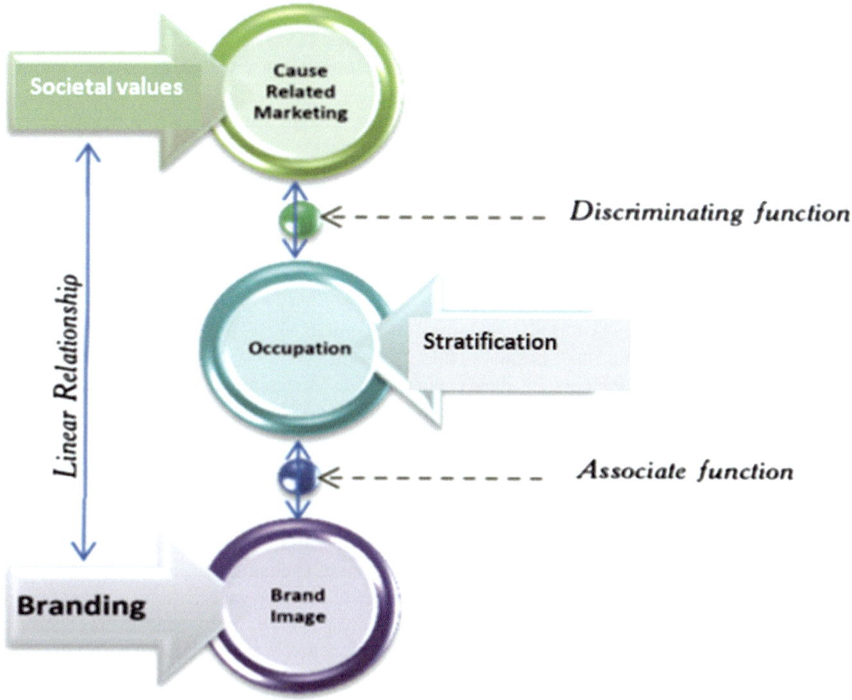

Fig. 2 Trivial relationship

To conclude, segmenting social-marketing activities is essential in fulfilling the social promise made to customers by leaders regarding diversity marketing, and this will yield social currency in the form of "brands of faith." Geo-demographic segmentation is the basis for segmenting, whereas to position the products, cause-related marketing strategies are needed to augment "brands of faith".

References

Anderson WT, Cunningham WH (1972) The socially conscious consumer. J Marketing 23–31
Aseem P (2002) Green marketing, public policy and managerial strategies
Chien-Hsiung L (2011) A study on the relations between the brand image and customer satisfaction in catering businesses. Afr J Bus Manage 5(18):7732–7739
Dahl DW, Moreau P (2002) The influence and value of analogical thinking during new product ideation. J Marketing Res 39(1):47–60
Driesener C, Romaniuk J (2006) Comparing methods of brand image measurement. Int J Market Res 48(6):681–698
Edelweiss Securities Report (2015) https://www.edelweiss.in/research
Guenther M-H (1992) Market and technology shifts in the 1990s: market fragmentation and mass customization. J Market Manage 303-314.

Hill RP, Ainscough T, Shank T, Manullang D (2009) Corporate social responsibility and socially responsible investing: a global perspective. J Bus Ethics 165–174

Hillier D, Jones P, Comfort D (2005) Corporate social responsibility and the UK's top ten retailers. Int J Retail Distrib manage 33(12):882–888

Hittner J, Pohle G (2008) Attaining sustainable growth through corporate social responsibility. IBM Global Business Services, United States of America

Jones P, Comfort D, Hillier D (2007) What's in store? Retail marketing and corporate social responsibility. Market Intel Plan 17–30

Majumdar S, Patel JP (2011) Does CSR really build brands? Marakathon 3(4):12–17

Paul Temporal's Branding Tips (2002) www.brandingasia.com

Peter K, Green Marketing (2008) Who's in Charge of Green? Advertising age (June 18). http://www.massogroup.com

Pivato S, Misani N, Tencati A (2008) The impact of corporate social responsibility on consumer trust: the case of organic food. business ethics, pp 3–12

Polonsky MJ (1995) A stakeholder theory approach to designing environmental marketing strategy. Unpublished Working Paper, Journal of Business and International Marketing, vol 10, pp 29–46

Popoli P (2011) Linking CSR strategy and brand image – Different approaches in local and global markets. Market Theor 419–433

Porter ME, Kramer MR (December 2006) Strategy and society: the link between competitive advantage and corporate social responsibility. Harward Business Review, pp 78–93

Raghavan P (2008) Fundamentals of Strategic Management. Dreamtech Press

Sengupta A (2008) Emergence of modern Indian retail: an historical perspective. Int J Retail Distrib Manage 36(9):689–700. Website of Isha Foundation: http://www.ishafoundation.org/?global

Weiser J, Zadek S Conversations with Disbelievers. USA. http://www.socialbusinessblog.com

Determinant Factors for the Formation and Development of a Smart Territory

Andra Zvirbule, Baiba Rivza and Zane Bulderberga

Abstract At present, the concept of regional development is based on the principles of planning, which involve smart growth and sustainable development. In most cases, a smart territory is understood as a sustainable and efficient territory that provides a high quality of life to its inhabitants through optimal management of its resources. In addition, this approach may be employed in identifying a smart territory and in the strategic planning of it as well as in the efficient use of resources in the territory. Most research studies focus on smart growth, which involves the sustainable use of resources, the development of the e-environment, solutions to urbanisation problems, waste management, environmental management, etc. However, few research studies are available on the factors determining a smart territory and their influence on territorial development. For this reason, research studies contributing to examining the groups of influencing factors in the aspect of formation of smart territories are important. In addition, the spectrum (i.e., types) of the factors is assumed to be very diverse. If it is assumed that smart growth and the formation of a smart territory is based on systems and subsystems that shape a complex perspective on the formation of a territory, such groups may involve not only the economic aspect but also the social, life quality, and sustainable community and business development aspects. The research aim is to identify the factors that influence the formation of a smart territory and to assess their effects on territorial development. The specific research tasks are as follows: (1) select the factors that influence the formation of a smart territory; and (2) assess the selected factors in terms of their influence on the development of a smart territory. Research methods employed include logical construction, monographic, focus-group analysis, and analytic hierarchy process.

Keywords Smart territory · Regional development · Smart growth · Knowledge economy

---

A. Zvirbule (✉) · B. Rivza · Z. Bulderberga
Faculty of Economics and Social Development, Latvia University of Agriculture University, Jelgava, Latvia
e-mail: Andra.Zvirbule@llu.lv
URL: http://www.llu.lv

E. Lau et al. (eds.), *Selected Papers from the Asia-Pacific Conference on Economics & Finance (APEF 2016)*, DOI 10.1007/978-981-10-3566-1_5

1 Introduction

A number of important strategic documents of the European Union place a certain focus on smart growth, the formation of smart territories, and the development of knowledge economies. In the EU's documents for the programming period 2014–2020, a special focus is placed on regional growth in accordance with the Research and Innovation Strategy for Smart Specialisation. However, examining the introduction of the smart-specialisation strategy in the EU's regions in 2015 revealed a number of factors that negatively influenced the development of smart specialisation. The problems were mostly associated with: (a) the regions' incapability to define their particular smart-specialisation priority area; (b) the regions' incapability to invest in additional measures of coordination (information management) among the government, regions, entrepreneurs, and residents; (c) the regions' incapability to enhance their knowledge on knowledge-economy strategies; (d) the regions' should find a better balance between planning and implementation activities; and (e) changes in the legislation of the regions/Member States hinder their decision making (Smart Specialisation Platform 2016). The report allows concluding that at the tactical and operational planning levels, there is no clarity regarding smart growth, smart specialization, as well as smart-territory development issues.

However, a number of researchers have focused their research on regional development not only on smart specialisation but also on the role of smart growth. For example, in their research on smart, sustainable, and inclusive regional growth and development, some scientists emphasize the role of the EU, national, and local governments in designing a conceptual model that integrates the role of technological advances, human capital and knowledge spillovers for economic growth and regional convergence. The research studies also stress regional disparities that must be taken into consideration when deciding on whether the region may be strategically defined and formed as a smart territory.

However, some researchers stress the existing problems in this aspect because economic development that is based on knowledge or a knowledge-based economy may not be viewed apart from the economic situation in a given territory. In addition, if associating a knowledge economy only with innovation, IT technologies, and businesses having a high capacity to use technologies, the most important factor—the quality of human resources, which contributes to the knowledge economy—is neglected (Karagiannis 2007).

Nevertheless, the contribution of human resources in particular is increasingly stressed in relation to smart territories and knowledge-based economies, which is interpreted as creative thinking that not only directly creates or gives economic benefits but also provides communication, perceiving new things, engaging in territorial development, and supporting ideas (Munro 2016).

The mentioned prerequisites and research findings underline the urgency and importance of the research topic, which is based on identifying and examining the factors that could form and develop smart territories.

For this reason, the authors defined their **research aim:** to identify factors that influence the formation of a smart territory and to assess their influences on territorial development.

The specific **research tasks** were as follows: (1) to select factors that influence the formation of a smart territory and (2) to assess the selected factors in terms of their influence on the development of a smart territory.

Research methods employed include logical construction, monographic, focus-group analysis, and the analytic hierarchy process.

2 Justification for the Selection of Factors Influencing the Formation and Development of a Smart Territory

While compiling and analysing the theoretical justification, a number of problem questions arise in the research process. If referring to one of the most important reports on smart specialisation, one could use the OECD's definition of the term "smart specialization": SMART specialisation is an industrial and innovation framework for regional economies that aims to illustrate how public policies, framework conditions, and especially R&D and innovation-investment policies can influence the economic, scientific, and technological specialisation of a region and consequently its path of productivity, competitiveness, and economic growth (Munro 2016). However, based on the European Commission's guidelines and strategy on smart specialisation, other terms and definitions are highlighted as well (The OECD Report 2013).

Smart specialisation strategies refer to regional strategies that "generate unique assets and capabilities based on a region's distinctive industrial structures and knowledge base." This concept is closely linked with the EU call for attention to "smart growth" strategies that are soundly based on knowledge and innovation and embedded in regions.

That is why the authors wished to summarise and interpret the various terms that refer to smart growth, smart territorial development, and knowledge-based economies (Table 1).

However, several researchers point that entrepreneurship-based innovations play a crucial role in the formation and development of a smart territory: Entrepreneurial actors are likely to play leading roles in discovering promising areas of future specialisation, not the least because the needed adaptations to local skills, materials, environmental conditions, and market access conditions are unlikely to be able to draw on codified, publicly shared knowledge but instead will entail gathering localized information and the formation of social capital assets (Foray et al. 2009).

In research studies, a smart territory currently transversally addresses fields as diverse as energy efficiency, information technology, transport infrastructure, resource consumption, or environmental impacts, among others (Garcia-Ayllon and Luis Miralles 2015). However, smart-territory indicators may be divided into the following categories according to their purpose of application (Table 2).

Table 1 Factors determining innovative, knowledge-based, and smart growth

Innovative growth	Knowledge-based growth	Smart growth
R&D investment Patents and patent application Product, process, organizational, and marketing innovation Innovative entrepreneurship	Share of highly educated workers Years of work experience Share of cognitive-skill workers Share of creative-class workers	Urbanisation economies (population density) Industrial specialization Amenity services—access to open space and diversified landscapes Climate conditions Creative communities—access to creative-class workers Presence of cross-industry activities such as tourism, food, drinks, etc. Cultural production External knowledge links—access to highly educated individuals Access to ICT, e.g., high-speed Internet Globally active firms

Source Authors' construction based on Sandu (2012), Naldi et al. (2015), McCann and Ortega-Argiles (2013)

Table 2 Smart-territory indicators and their purpose of application

Indicators	Purpose of smart territorial development
Number of partners involved in territorial networks for development projects Variation of number of interregional cooperation projects Gini coefficient on social polarization	Governance development
Number of people employed in R&D Private/public enterprises in GDP spending on research and development Number of researchers/1000 employees	Research and development
Relationship between agricultural land used for organic production and the total UAA employed population in primary sector/region population	Crisis of rural development
Number of cultural heritage sites with a management plan or plan for their use Impact of tourism & industry impact	Landscape management
Industrial production index: percentage of investment in capital goods Existence of incentives for enterprises Percentage of active population with higher-education qualifications (i.e., university degrees and higher-level vocational training certificates)	Sustainability of regional economic resources

Source Authors' construction based on Garcia-Ayllon and Luis Miralles (2015)

In identifying and developing a smart territory, the necessity for several priority areas or focuses is determined both by the territorial planning aspect, which is important for progress in the national economy, and by the opinion of local governments about the vision at local level. A number of regional and territorial development researchers point that smart development is not a one size-fits-all concept, and its application in rural contexts must be combined with a place-based approach adjusted to fit the specifics of rural contexts and linkages (Naldi et al. 2015; Asheima and Coenena 2005; Bell and Jayne 2010; Rusua 2013). They stress that some regions and territories are in the "crouching start" position to rapidly introduce or follow smart-territory principles. It is justified by the fact that these regions have some general characteristics that limit their potential to gain from smart-growth policies such as lack of scale in their population and industrial base and limited access to markets. However, focusing more on, or smartly/wisely exploiting, resources that would considerably contribute to the knowledge capacity of a territory/region is suggested as a solution. It is also stressed that smart growth may be achieved through exploiting local amenities as well.

However, if assessing a smart territory based on the principles of knowledge-based entrepreneurship, one may face a number of discussible assumptions about territorial development on the whole. Such an aspect is emphasised by Stefan Trzcielinski in his research investigations. He points out that innovative and knowledge-based entrepreneurship is influenced by exogenous factors; in addition, the mechanism of this influence is a complicated multifactor aggregate (Trzcielinski 2015). The author mentions the following most important factors: overall performance of the economy, the economic regime, the innovation system, education, labour, and information and communication technology. However, he further adds that each of the factors form a criteria group. These factors have the most significant influence on entrepreneurship and shaping the brightness, flexibility, intelligence, and shrewdness of an enterprise.

3 Hierarchy of Factors Influencing the Formation and Development of a Smart Territory and Their Evaluation

Based on theoretical findings (The role of clusters in smart specialization strategies 2013), local government recommendations, national strategic priorities, entrepreneur interests, as well as the authors' opinions, the present research involves forming a hierarchy of factors and identifying its focuses (Fig.1).

The hierarchy of factors was created to assess and determine the formation and development of a smart territory. Level 1 involved the factor groups that make the most significant influence on the formation and development of a smart territory. The factor groups are as follows:

(1) residents
(2) local governments
(3) the national government
(4) the European Union

Level 2 systems, which represent a more detailed division of influences of the factor groups, were determined and selected for the hierarchy's factor groups. Level 3 involves particular alternative priority areas that allow identifying a smart territory's progress based on specific indications. The priority areas selected are as follows:

(1) future: planning/funding-based development
(2) space: resource-based development
(3) people: cooperation-based development
(4) products: innovation- and entrepreneurship-based development

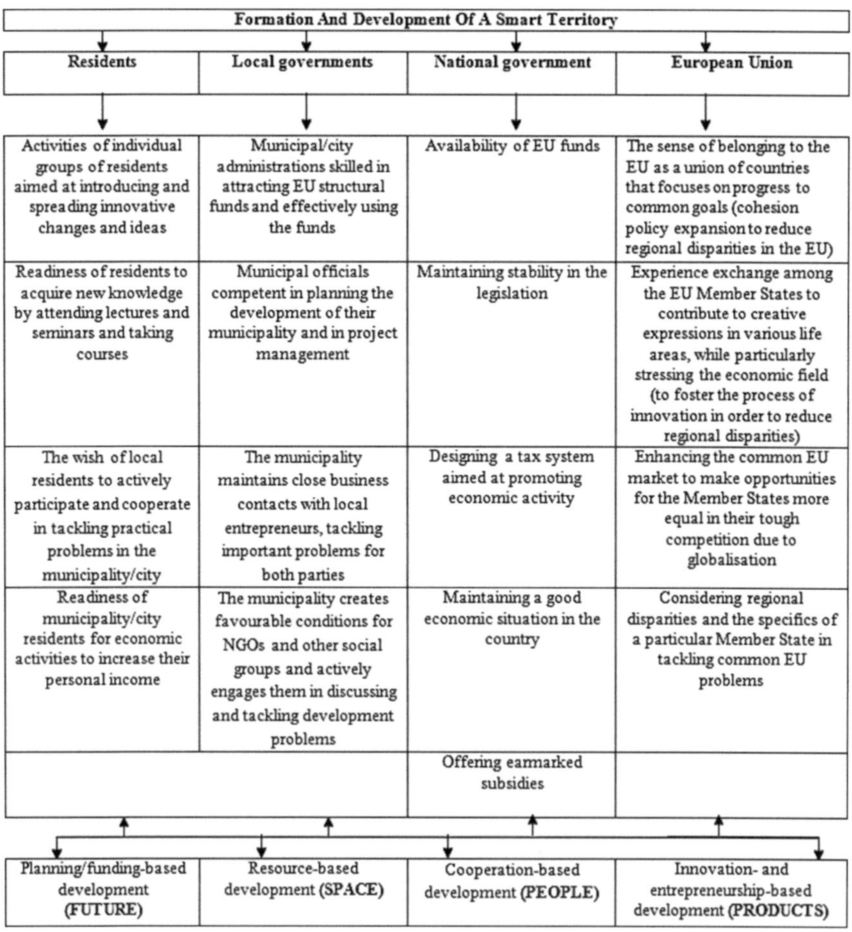

Fig. 1 Hierarchy composition for the formation and development of a smart territory (Authors construction)

Furthermore, a group of experts was established ($n = 16$): The experts represented the interests of all of the priority areas and factors involved in the hierarchy composition. The experts' group was made up as follows: 20% were heads of municipalities; 20% represented the interests of residents and had experience in establishing NGOs and holding local resident activities contributing to regional growth; 20% represented applied research organisations and business interests; and 20% were high-qualification scientists in the field of regional development.

The hierarchy composition was created based on a discussion with the experts and the role of level 1 factors assessed performing AHP pairwise comparisons. Analytic hierarchy process (AHP) is a basic approach to decision making. It is designed to cope with both the rational and the intuitive to select the best from a number of alternatives evaluated with respect to several criteria. In this process, the decision maker carries out simple pairwise comparison judgments, which are then used to develop overall priorities for ranking the alternatives. The evaluations were based on the distribution and explanation of a relative scale (Table 3).

The expert evaluations were summarized; average-priority vector values were calculated for each factor group; and minimum and maximum values were determined. The following equation was employed to make the pairwise comparisons and to calculate the priority vector values (Eq. 1).

$$\begin{pmatrix} \frac{w_1}{w_1} & \frac{w_1}{w_2} & \cdots & \frac{w_1}{w_n} \\ \frac{w_2}{w_1} & \frac{w_2}{w_2} & \cdots & \frac{w_2}{w_n} \\ \vdots & \vdots & \ddots & \vdots \\ \frac{w_n}{w_1} & \frac{w_n}{w_2} & \cdots & \frac{w_n}{w_n} \end{pmatrix} \begin{pmatrix} w_1 \\ w_2 \\ \vdots \\ w_n \end{pmatrix} = n \begin{pmatrix} w_1 \\ w_2 \\ \vdots \\ w_n \end{pmatrix} \tag{1}$$

Table 3 Relative importance scale (Saaty 1990)

Intensity of importance	Definition	Explanation
1	Equal importance	Two activities contribute equally to the objective
2	Weak or slight	
3	Moderate importance	Experience and judgment slightly favour one activity over another
4	Moderate plus	
5	Strong importance	Experience and judgment strongly favour one activity over another
6	Strong plus	
7	Very strong or demonstrated importance	An activity is favoured very strongly over another; its dominance is demonstrated in practice
8	Very, very strong	
9	Extreme importance	The evidence favouring one activity over another is of the highest possible order of affirmation

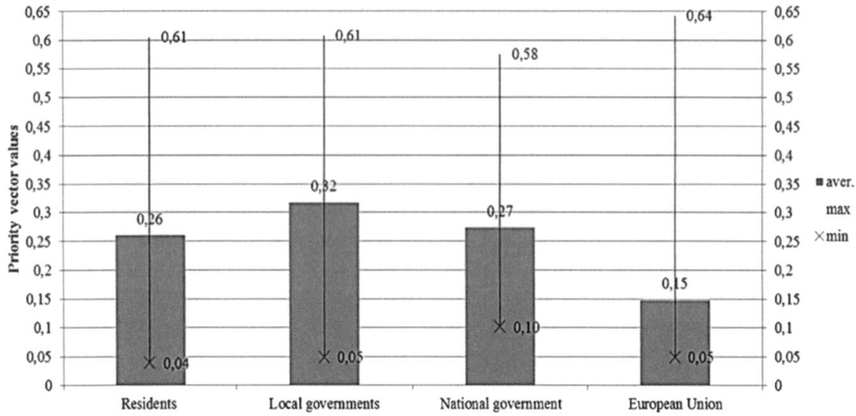

Fig. 2 Overall priorities for Level 1 factor groups including differences between minimum and maximum vector values given by the experts (n = 16)

The results acquired are presented in Fig. 2.

According to the experts, the strongest factor group influencing the formation and development of a smart territory was the factor group "local governments" with an average priority vector value of 0.32. The values for the factor groups "residents" and "national government" were quite similar (0.26 and 0.27, respectively). The experts gave a lower evaluation value (0.15) to the factor group "European Union." A common feature of the expert evaluations, which might be viewed as hindering making a consistent decision on the most important criteria groups, was the lack of unanimity among the experts. As seen in Fig. 2, there are large differences between the minimum and maximum priority vector values for the factor groups. The greatest expert disagreement was observed regarding the factor group "European Union" because the experts had very diverse opinions about this factor group's influence on the formation and development of a smart territory. In contrast, the greatest expert unanimity was observed regarding the factor group "national government." The research result for Level 1 factor groups and their evaluation values will be employed to examine Level 2 factors based on global-priority vector calculations.

4 Conclusions

(1) After examining the recommendations on national and regional development and growth developed by the EU and the European Commission, one can conclude that at the tactical and operational planning levels, there is no clarity regarding smart growth, smart specialization, as well as smart-territory development issues.

(2) In identifying and developing a smart territory, the necessity for several priority areas or focuses is determined both by the territorial planning aspect, which is important for progress in the national economy, and by the opinion of local governments about the vision at local level.
(3) To assess and determine the formation and development of a smart territory, a hierarchy of influencing factors may be created, which is composed of two levels and defines four alternative priority areas: future, space, people and products.
(4) According to the experts, the strongest factor group that influenced the formation and development of a smart territory was the factor group "local governments" with an average priority vector value of 0.32. The values for the factor groups "residents" and "national government" were quite similar (0.26 and 0.27, respectively). The experts gave a lower evaluation value (0.15) to the factor group "European Union."
(5) For further research, it is useful to continue to evaluate the hierarchy's factors, focusing on Level 2 factors, which would involve global-priority vector calculations.

Acknowledgements The paper was prepared in the framework of the National Research programme EKOSOC-LV as the part of subproject 5.2.3 "Rural and Regional Development Processes and Opportunities in Latvia in the Context of Knowledge Economy".

References

Asheima BT, Coenena L (2005) Knowledge bases and regional innovation systems: comparing Nordic clusters. Res Policy 34(8):1173–1190

Bell D, Jayne M (2010) The creative countryside: policy and practice in the UK rural cultural economy. J Rural Stud 26:209–218. doi:10.1016/j.jrurstud.2015.06.006

Foray D, David P, Hall B (2009) Smart specialisation—the concept, knowledge economists policy brief. http://ec.europa.eu/invest-in-research/pdf/download_en/kfg_policy_brief_no9.pdf?11111

Garcia-Ayllon S, Luis Miralles J (2015) New strategies to improve governance in territorial management: evolving from "smart cities" to "smart territories". Procedia Eng 118:3–11. doi:10.1016/j.proeng.2015.08.396

Karagiannis S (2007) The knowledge-based economy, convergence and economic growth: evidence from the European Union. J Econ Asymmetries 4(2):65–85. doi:10.1016/j.jeca.2007.02.005

McCann P, Ortega-Argiles R (2013) Smart specialization, regional growth and applications to European Union cohesion policy. http://www.tandfonline.com/doi/abs/10.1080/00343404.2013.79976

Munro E (2016) Illuminating the practice of knowledge exchange as a 'pathway to impact' within an arts and humanities research council 'creative economy knowledge exchange' project. Geoforum 71:44–51

Naldi L, Nilsson P, Westlund H, Wixe S (2015) What is smart rural development? J Rural Stud 40:90–101

Rusua M (2013) Smart specialization a possible solution to the new global challenges. Procedia Econ and Financ 6:128–136

Saaty TL (1990) The analytic hierarchy process. McGraw Hill, New York

Sandu S (2012) Smart specialization concept and the status of its implementation in Romania, emerging markets queries in finance and business. Procedia Econ Financ 3:236–242. doi:10.1016/S2212-5671(13)00124-X

Smart Specialisation Platform (2016) http://s3platform.jrc.ec.europa.eu/en/knowledge-repository

The OECD Report (2013) Innovation-driven growth in regions: the role of smart specialization. http://www.oecd.org/sti/inno/smartspecialisation.htm

The role of clusters in smart specialization strategies (2013) https://ec.europa.eu/research/…/pdf/…/clusters_smart_spec2013.pdf

Trzcielinski S (2015) The influence of knowledge based economy on agility of enterprise. Procedia Manufact 3:6615–6623. doi:10.1016/j.promfg.2015.11.001

Replacing Formal Authority in the Workplace with Employee Self-governing Authority

Juan Nicolás Montoya Monsalve, Álvaro Fernando Moncada Niño and Juan Daniel Montoya Naranjo

Abstract A number of authors throughout organizational history have raised the importance of establishing authority—addition to top management—in an organization, thus creating a flow domain as well as a responsibility to sort through the different resources with the sole intention to make the organization efficient and highly profitable. This has been done from the praxis, epistemology, ontology, and a number of other points of view; however, the concept of leadership has been distorted by confusing authority with the command, obligation, and strength needed for resource management and jurisdiction. Meanwhile, formal authority has suffered serious transformations in organizations, although the discussion of its components is widely supported by the bureaucratic theory, its integration into the administrative process, and proactive business development. This transformation has been defined and made manifest by the decline in the exercise of authority, which contributes to the formulation of generosity, commitment, and engagement, thus promoting the development of high-performance practices in human-resource management and turns people into its strategic and competitive components. From the experience gained in different companies in Latin America, which has been categorized as a "great place to work," through modeling based on effectiveness and devoid of the concept of authority, the system has allowed research to determine the effect of formal authority as nonrecurring businesses gain a more flexible and adaptive element in terms of recognizing the ability of individuals, their knowledge, and their willingness to belong to a particular organization. The nonhierarchical design, the effects of structural position in organizations, the impact of leadership, the relationship of structures and charges in connection with the successes and achievements of the organization, the impact on relationships and communication, authoritarian imposition, noncooperation along with the lack of consistency with

J.N.M. Monsalve (✉) · J.D.M. Naranjo
National University of Colombia (Manizales), Manizales, Colombia
e-mail: jdmontoya08@hotmail.com

Á.F.M. Niño
Center for Higher Management Studies (CESA), Bogotá, Colombia

E. Lau et al. (eds.), *Selected Papers from the Asia-Pacific Conference on Economics & Finance (APEF 2016)*, DOI 10.1007/978-981-10-3566-1_6

individual purposes, the mission and the Provisional Record, continuous bad decisions, relationships with management and control finally all connect these elements with the actual individuals of the organization who are immersed in a knowledge society.

Keywords Hierarchy · Authority · Power · Pyramid structure · Subordination · Competitiveness · Job performance · Managing for results · Self-sufficient · Self-critical · Self-commitment · Authors · Flexibility · Adaptability

1 Introduction

The discipline of human-resource management has been criticized for its lack of theoretical frameworks that serve as a foundation both for scientific research and the development of a common doctrine. This has been modified by recent researchers who have made great efforts to model conceptually different studies carried out through various theories of the organization.

These models attempt to analyze the relationship between business strategy, human resource-management, and business performance through three different approaches:

(1) Contingent approach, whereby a relationship between HRM and strategy influences the results. The independent and moderating variables are addressed by the theory based on resources and capabilities or the industrial economy.
(2) Universalist focus, which defends the existence of certain practices that always contribute to an improvement in business performance regardless of the strategic option chosen.
(3) Configurative approach, which is an intermediate position in which there is no difference between the independent variable and the moderator variable: Both are equally important. This approach emphasizes the importance of the relationship "I" to enter the elements of the organization (holistic approach).

The problem that arises is that there are no conclusive studies. On the contrary, we find it difficult to obtain clear and unanimous findings to help build a single framework for the management of human resources. We found differences between the practices that are defined as high involvement or high performance, as is the operationalization of competitive strategy, which causes an imprecise fit between strategy and commitment by management. Moreover, most of these studies have focused on analyzing only operational practices and techniques of human-resource management such that their level of study is too superficial, leaving aside the true policy and principles of human-resource management. We also found conflicting results when analyzing the consistency between strategy and business management.

In addition, there is little empirical evidence that such adjustment is necessary or even beneficial because the results are inconclusive.

Therefore, this work represents a first approach to the study of three elements as follows: (1) the principles influencing the management system being in line with strategic choices; and (2) high-performance practices in human-resource management and business performance. Focusing on the configurative approach and taking as a given the company study, we analyze the impact it has on the decreased use of formal authority (such as business principle) in the choice of practices and techniques of high-performance human-resource management and the impact on business results. This will seek to integrate the contingent and universalist approaches by analyzing their literature and to determine the possible existence of a direct relationship between the two.

2 Formal Authority as a Restriction on "Steering"

The exercise of formal authority, i.e., Taylorism, as promulgated by the unique method of coordination, has been used through times of great difficulty in modern organizations. The increase in educational level, which gives a greater approach and leads to the demand of a greater role in decisions; the increased living standards in developed countries; the decreased economic dependence of the subject and, consequently, increased power over organizations; the increased complexity of the operation of enterprises, which requires close coordination of efforts among professionals; the increased awareness of human dignity, which leads to forsaking for more participation, more development, or change in the organizational structure, which has become more complex; and the increased autonomy: All of these have led to the concept of the subordinate, which has been modified a partner or teammate and favors recognition that inflexibility hurts the performance of the organization itself.

For this reason, the responsibilities of the subjects are not only those described in the job description but are also those that are set according to the capabilities of the workers, thus simplifying the levels of organizational hierarchy and giving rise to "flatter" organization charts. One can also see how one begins to implement new ways of working such as telecommuting, job decentralization, collective work, and other dynamics that support the mobility of labor.

The functional development of the human factor arises in the search for strategic development. This will generate a new concept and the chain of command—whether bureaucratic, plutocratic, or more dynamic forms such as heterarchy, empowerment, self-management or to, for instance, a holonarquía consensual democracy. Thus, this leads to an organization called a "coalition," in which there is no hierarchical relationship because it is self-managed because each member has certain responsibilities and has discretion over the resources he or she controls; therefore, the remuneration is determined ex-post depending on the group's results.

The coalition raises two major problems of organizational design that human-resources management must solve: coordination and incentives. Coordination is needed because of the existence of interdependencies between the decisions of the players, plus sharing of information is necessary to enable each member to anticipate the decisions or actions of others or to establish ex-ante routines or decision rules. Culture can be considered as a mechanism that restricts the conduct of its members and facilitates coordination, which at the time it is passed down to whomever will be interested that it is the only course of action to follow when reaching decisions on issues that have not been covered previously. Cremer states precisely the mechanisms through which culture enhances coordination and provides the following two: (1) the common language, which facilitates communication; and (2) the establishment of rules of conduct such that each member can predict the behavior of others and adjust their own behavior. In the same direction, Kreeps emphasizes the use of culture as a coordinating mechanism especially when individual behavior can lead to multiple equilibriums effects. There is also evidence that management style and corporate culture are intimately related aspects of system management, and human resources can argue that only through the consistency between them can one generate sustainable competitive advantages over the long term. This idea is also found in the work of Ogboma and Harris and that of Hemey when they argue, respectively, that how leadership style affects performance is itself influenced by corporate culture and propose corporate culture as a requirement for the success of a particular leadership style.

From all of this follows the following proposition:

P1: A decrease in business formal authority should be replaced by a business culture strongly oriented toward interpersonal relationships to enhance collaboration and commitment between worker and the organization.

3 Impact on Human-Resources Management: Practices of High Commitment

High-involvement management has also been described as "high-performance practices" (Huselid 1995) and is also known as soft model of HRM. However, basically this is an approach to a human resources management–oriented commitment to employees and involves their active participation in decision-making, providing resources, and providing the organizational support necessary to do so (Valle et al. 2000).

Although have been richly described in the literature, the problem arises in determining which practices of specific human-resources management enhance and serve to monitor engagement because studies show no unanimity on the issue. To determine high-commitment practices, some authors recommend first that measuring the degree to which the concept of human resources is a part of management (i.e., commitment to management) or, in the terms of Eisenberger, that those engagements that must be observed and measured determine the organizational support received by the employee.

Unanimity is found in that autonomy of workers is emphasized over the product of their work, thereby increasing experimentation and promoting internal communication and coordination among different members of the organization. The two main arguments that have been established for the incorporation of these high-commitment practices include the following: (1) They allow the organization to be more effective; and (2) they increases the social approval of this model as opposed to traditional Taylorist style, which is based on the strict control and subordination of employees. Thus, one can say that high-commitment practices are positively related to the decreased use of formal authority by companies, which allows us to make the following proposition:

P2: With the lower use of formal authority, companies can use high-commitment practices to manage their human resources and achieve greater business results.

4 Methodology

This paper presents some aspects of the case study as a research method in management science. It is based on the method as a way of generating theories about complex causal organizational phenomena. The correct application of this research tool legitimizes and encourages the use of its results, thus facilitating the connection between academia and industry. "The rationality of administrative tasks is a practice that uses rational technical tools and prudently considers its validity and feasibility, bearing in mind the specific cultural and historical circumstances and, above all, the personality of those who constitute the firm. Hence, the case method appears as an extremely suitable for teaching".

Investigation cases generally adopt an integrated perspective. A case study is, as defined by Yin (1994), "empirical research that examines a contemporary phenomenon within its real life context, especially when the boundaries between phenomenon and context are not clearly evident (…) A case study research successfully treated with technically distinctive situation in which there are many more variables of interest to observational data and, as a result, based on multiple sources of evidence, with data that must converge in a style of triangulation, and also as a result, benefits from prior development of theoretical propositions to guide data collection and data analysis."

Popper wrote that the case-study method, as well as statistical and other quantitative approaches, seeks to develop theories with empirically verifiable consequences. The case-study method proposed provides generalization and inference to the theory and not to other cases within the case, thus aiming to introduce quantitative data to consolidate the qualitative findings.

Mitchell agrees that then the logical inference is epistemologically quite independent of statistical inference. In terms of the canons of statistical inference, the analyst can assume that the same relationship exists between the same characteristics in the parent population. However, the inference from the sample relative to the parent population is drawn simply on the concomitant variation of the two characteristics. Given the logical inference (some call it "scientific" or "causal"), the researcher postulates or discovers relationships between features in the context of an explanatory conceptual framework. The relevance of the case and its generalization does not come, then, from the statistical side but rather from the logical side and thus the characteristics of the case study be extrapolated to other cases on the strength of explanatory reasoning.

A research design is composed of following five components according to Yin (1994):

1. the questions of the study,
2. the authors' proposals, if any,
3. the unit of analysis (several times),
4. the logic linking the data with the proposals, and
5. the criteria by which the findings are interpreted.

Oriented propositions about the objects to be examined in the study include captious questions of why and how to determine what to study. From the research questions, systematic data are sought to draw conclusions. The questions, data, and conclusions are logically linked together by the case design.

Some authors, such as Dyer, are inclined to study of a single case and cite support for one's position, e.g. classics such as Street Corner Society, which shows the importance of focusing an in-depth study of a single case. Others, such as Eisenhardt, argue instead that it is possible to obtain resources for multiple cases; in fact, there are examples of multiple classics such as Crozier. Smith relates that in his experience, as each case progresses through interviews, the data adapts to a pattern, in other words, a theory emerges, and successive data are predictable from the theory.

5 The Case Analysis[1]: SEMCO

SEMCO is a company that has attracted unprecedented interest around the world for its innovative practices in managing its resources, in particular, human resources, which led it to become the largest manufacturing company for marine and-food processing machinery in Brazil. SEMCO treats its 800 employees as responsible adults. Created in 1953 by an Austrian-born engineer, Antonio Curt Semler. SEMCO focuses its production activities in five factories producing a range of sophisticated products including marine pumps, digital scanners, commercial dish washers, filters for trucks, and mixing equipment for everything from gum to rocket fuel. Its main clients include Alcoa, Saab, and General Motors. Semler has built several factories cookies for Nabisco, Nestle, and United Biscuits. SEMCO's multinational competitors include AMF, Worthington Industries, Mitsubishi Heavy Industries, and Carrier.

The founder guided his son, Ricardo Semler, who had to deal with difficult regarding his county's economy and the fate of SEMCO. Apparently health problems resulting from stress placed Ricardo in a position of passivity, which led him to accept the proposed self-management of SEMCO's workers. To avoid massive layoffs and tying employee compensation to company profits, while cutting the pay of executives, Ricardo Semler later organized and coordinated small units (≤ 200 employees) under the conditions of decreased staff and rotating CEO (the position rotates every 6 months) and owner. However, undoubtedly the most interesting scenario in this development is that each individual could set their wages, set their working hours, was focused on making democratic decisions and largely autonomous divisions, which are specified in a small survival manual. All of these changes led to SEMCO being a unorthodox company that makes large amounts of money by avoiding decisions, rules, and executive authority. Everyone has access to the company books, and all workers cast a vote on important corporate decisions.

Management Associations, unions, and the press repeatedly pointed out SEMCO as the best company to work for in Brazil. No jobs are advertised, however, until 300 applications are received for each available position.

SEMCO has three fundamental values on which some 30 administrative programs are based. These values—democracy, profit sharing, and information—work together synergistically with each depending on the other two. The corporate structure, the freedom of employees, the relations with the union, and the limitations on the size of the factory: All of these elements are the product of commitment to these principles.

The first of the three values of SEMCO is democracy or employee engagement. Clearly employees who control their working conditions are happier than those who do not. Implementing employee engagement is a complex issue, so difficult and usually so frustrating that it's easier to talk about it than to carry it out. SEMCO

[1]For a more complete view of Semco Group and its activities, see http://www.semco.locaweb.com.br.

found four major obstacles to effective participatory management: size, hierarchy, lack of motivation, and ignorance. In a vast production unit, people feel small, unknown, and unable to influence the way work is done or the final utility obtained.

The organizational pyramid is the cause of much damage the companies because the journey from the base to the top is too long. Organizational pyramids emphasize power, promote insecurity, distort communications, hamper interaction, and make it difficult for people who plan and execute policies affecting people who move in the same direction. SEMCO then designed an organizational circle. Its greatest advantage is to decrease the number of levels of government to three: a corporate level and two operational levels in the manufacturing units.

The main circle consists of three concentric circles. A small central circle consists of five movements that integrate the company. The second circle, a larger circle, represents the heads of eight divisions; the so-called "partners." Finally, a third, a huge circle contains all other employees. Most of them are what are called "associates" and are responsible for research, design, sales, and manufacturing work and not have anyone to report them regularly. However, some of them are on a permanent or temporary team where their role is to lead, and are they called "coordinators." No manager reports to another coordinator, and that feature of the system is bringing about a decrease in management layers.

No one is selected or promoted until he or she has been interviewed and accepted by all future subordinates. Twice per year, subordinate managers are evaluated. In addition, twice per year everyone in the company performs due diligence in an anonymous questionnaire regarding the company's credibility and the competence of senior management. Among other things, employees are asked what things would make them quit or go on strike. SEMCO insists on making important decisions in a collegial manner, and certain decisions are made after a general vote in the company, which calls for participatory management.

Other ways to combat the hierarchy is to give employees control over their own lives. In short, adults are recruited and then treated as adults. Common sense is a risky tactic because it requires personal responsibility.

SEMCO has no rules about dress. The idea that personal appearance is important in a job, any job, is considered is silly. A company that needs business clothes to prove their seriousness probably has no significant profit that promotes and insists on job rotation every 2–5 years to avoid discouragement.

On the experimental side, SEMCO has a program for people who are trained in entry-level skills: It is called "Lost in Space" and select a couple of people each year who do not have a job description. The have a sponsor for 1 year and can do whatever they want while working in at least 12 different areas or units. By the same logic that governs the other programs for employees, clocks have been removed. Employees come and go according to their own schedules, even on the factory floor. When flexible working hours were introduced, it was decided to conduct regular follow-up meetings to identify problems and decide how to handle excess and work stoppages. This happened years ago, and the first of these meetings have occurred. The employees form groups, but they find their own leaders. And this is not due to lack of structure, just lack of a structure imposed from "above."

At SEMCO, each division has an individual profit-sharing program. Twice per year calculates 23% of the profits after taxes; enters the result on the income statement in each division; and give a check to three employees who have been elected by those working in that division. These three workers invest the money until each unit can meet and decide, by simple majority vote, what to do with the money. In most of the units, this is decided by an equal distribution. If the unit has 150 employees, the total is divided by 150 and a portion is given to each employee. It's that simple. Whoever sweeps the floor receives the same amount as the partner. Many things contribute to a successful profit-sharing program: low employee turnover, competitive pay, lack of paternalism, refusal to grant consolation prizes when profits fall, frequent distribution of earnings, and many opportunities for employees to challenge management decisions affecting future profits. However, nothing is more important than those frequent, brief, and honest vital statistics reports about the company's performance: There is total transparency, no tricks, and no simplifications.

All employees of SEMCO attend classes to learn to read and understand the company "numbers," and one of its unions transcribes the classes. Each month, each employee receives a balance sheet, a profit-and-loss analysis, and a statement of the cash flow in their division. Reports contain approximately 70 items (more, incidentally, than those who used to run the company, but SEMCO do not want anyone to think that it is withholding information). The actual figures always show positive long-term consequences.

What matters in the budget as well as the reports is that the numbers are few and important and that employees understand the approach to them. And that's all. Participation gives people control over their work; profit sharing gives them a reason to perform better; and information tells them what works and what does not.

6 Measurement Variables

Use of formal authority:

- Number of hierarchical levels or responsibility
- Language used: subordinate versus "roommate"
- Rules and guidelines: Focus on power or responsibility
- Centres of decision: One versus multiple
- Decision-making: Individual versus collective

Variables measuring organizational support as perceived by employees:

- Management puts into place actions to identify resources and information needs of all personnel in the company
- Management communicates and formally recognizes staff achievements

- Management formally announces the company's policies and strategy to all employees
- Managers and supervisors allow employees to have a high degree of autonomy and self-control over their actions

High-commitment human-resources practices:

- Staffing is selective: Management seeks individuals who fit the organization and its culture, not the other way around.
- Fixed contracts: The use of permanent contracts is set in a policy of stable employment or temporary contracts.
- Intensive training: Many training opportunities are available to employees or
- Generic training: Multipurpose oriented training enables employees to develop different functions and correct defects in performance.
- Promotion qualitative: The use of promotion criteria based on attitudes that support the organizational culture or quantitative promotion.
- Qualitative assessment: The use of evaluation criteria based on attitudes that support the organizational culture or quantitative assessment.
- Remuneration is based on an individual base salary, which is determined by the knowledge of individuals and their flexibility to perform multiple tasks or based on the job requirements.
- Level of medium-to-high compensation: Salary levels are at or above the market average, and external equity is sought.
- Long-term compensation: Incentive pay is linked to the achievement of objectives over the medium to long term.
- Incentive groups: Collective performance (e.g., work teams, company) is the criterion for the allocation of incentive pay or individual incentives.

Variables considered in measuring results:

- Improvement in financial results
- Increased market share
- Improved earnings as a percentage of sales
- Increased sales per employee
- Performance in the workplace
- High-quality troubleshooting
- Levels of turnover and absenteeism

7 Conclusions

Today the concept of authority is limited the procedures for making decisions have come down to lower corporate levels. The hierarchical system that was used previously has given rise to a system in which employees are responsible for their own actions, and leadership comes from the teams and not just one person as it previously did.

Traditional formal authority is not effective because orders can be disobeyed as often they are obeyed even when they are wrong, and the consequences of these give rise to different possibilities. Authority rests on the acceptance (or not) of the consent and approval of subordinates, so there is in fact the concept of legitimacy of authority, but it is very simple: People simply choose between different subordinate alternatives to obey or not obey. It is important that the organizational structure helps to create a situation in which the administrator can manage more effectively. In this sense, the organization is a technique to foster leadership. If the assignment of authority and structural arrangements creates a situation where there is a tendency for heads of departments to be viewed as leaders and which help them in their leadership tasks, this will prove organizational structure to be an essential element.

This perspective implicitly posits an opposition between heterarchical (identified by those that occur in networks) and hierarchical relations (associated with chains of authority). The latter appear as harmful and to be banished or as the expression of a form of lower—or somewhat inadequate to meet the demands of the global economy and contemporary economic societies—organization. All members of an organization have the authority to make decisions and take actions that affect the future of the organization. One of the contributions of the new concept of authority focus on the technical revolution to make decisions, and that does not correspond to organizational subjects but rather to dynamic outside hierarchical structures.

There may be circumstances in which a team leader makes a sensible decision, but to others it does not. Moreover, sometimes, performance decreases head, because low motivation. It must be accountable to oneself and not to the manager in this sense that there is a recognition of the autonomy of the labor force and clarity of the items contracted beyond subordination.

Some might argue that leaders are needed to decide what the general direction should be. The question to ask then is this: How many DGs are leaders of their teams, and is this absence simplified by the hierarchical structure, delegation, and the imposition of subordinate status?

These assumptions lead one to think that modern or contemporary companies are already far from requiring hierarchical environments because people and organizations have evolved cognitively and competitively, some not even requiring new forms of government, but better ways to address government. In this sense, new models and practices should aim at simplifying the reduction of complexity in the organizational world, trying to be consistent with real-world processes, and being relevant to the objectives of each employee in building the capacity for dynamic interactive learning about different processes and forms of Interdependence, causal attributions of responsibility and capacity to act, and opportunities for coordination in a complex and turbulent environment.

This capacity is improved when agents can move from one to another of the various modes of governance for more a effective responses to internal or external turbulence, in developing methods for coordinating activities among different identities of social forces, interests and systems with different meanings in different spatio-temporal horizons, and different areas of intervention. This depends on the self-reflective use of self-organization to support the exchange, negotiation, or solidarity—as well as the specific nature of coordination problems that may arise when acting at different scales and in different time horizons—to determine a common world view and a system that stabilizes the orientations, expectations, and standards of behavior of key actors. This can be carried out with a systematic analysis and assessment of problems and opportunities, availability and resource requirements, and the framework for the continuing fulfillment of coordination both positive and negative.

8 Other Conclusions

- Employees must be trained general way to operate at full capacity and not only in terms of specific functions. Coordination and leadership are not the same type of authority.
- The organizational structure, not the authority, can be adapted to contingent structures in terms of knowledge (professional, empirical, formal, or informal).
- Hierarchical relationships (as proposed by many members with power and authority) decrease the effectiveness of organizations.
- Authority and power lines do not energize the organization and thus are not essential.
- Employees react negatively to a lack of authority in organizations, e.g., resulting in dismissals, disciplinary procedures, absenteeism, turnover, etc.
- Companies do not consider employees as a single body, in which all members have the same goals, but rather as the mission and vision of the organization.
- Small and large organizations will have the same application under authority and function, or they will simply state that it is not required.
- The new organizational theories tend to express autonomy, but the inability of people make them work, which is usually accomplished through hierarchy, domination, subordination, and authority, hinders their ability to do so.
- A lack of rigid and hierarchical structures does not mean that things are chaotic.
- Authority represents an organizing principle and nothing else.
- An education in confidence is one of the most important values of society and a kind of success for the future. It is a real accomplishment to survive the management of a new business.
- Authority is distributed throughout the organization.
- Fear is a symptom of the loss of power and authority.
- The dissident restores the dignity of the employee, prevents the deterioration of physical qualities, maintains intellectual and emotional autonomy, and holds the status quo of the companies.

- Assuming that authority lies in the hierarchy, there should be no difference between leaders and managers.
- Maximizing individual human utility depends on their resources and production.

References

Barcelona, Gestión 2000 y Aedipe. (52–54) (1998) La Ecuación humana. Cómo diseñar y dirigir empresas de alto rendimiento.123. Gestión 2000. Barcelona, p 315

Bennett J (1993) Review of: understanding whole language, by Constance Weaver, pp 46–47

Bennis WG (1969) Leadership and motivation. Addison Wesley Publishing Company, Reading, p 286

Bennis WG (1976) Organization development in transition. J Appl Behav Sci 12(1):22–43

Bofill J (1950) La escala de los seres o el dinamismo de la perfección. Cristiandad, Barcelona

Deming E (1989) Calidad, productividad y competitividad. Díaz de Santos, Madrid

Giménez GY, Simon B (2002) Una Nueva Perspectiva en la Medición del capital Humano. Departamento de Estructura, Historia Económica y Economía Publica, Universidad de Zaragoza, Documento de Trabajo N° 2 (Febrero), pp 1–28

Hagen A et al (1998) Critical strategic leadership components: an empirical investigation. Adv Manag J 63

Hall RH (1996) Organizaciones: estructuras, procesos y resultados. Prentice-Hall Hispanoamericana, México, D.F., pp 120–122

Hammer M, Champy J (1993) Reengineering the corporation: a manifesto for businness revolution. Harper Collins Publishers Inc. New York

Ishikawa K (1988). Qué es el control de Calidad? (la modalidad japonesa). Ed. Revolucionaria, La Habana

Kaplan RS, Norton DP (1992) The balanced scorecard: measures that drive performance. Harvard Bus Rev 70(1):71–79

Lusthaus C et al (1999) Capacity development: definitions, issues and implications for planning, monitoring and evaluation. Universalia Occasional No. 35, Sept 1999, p 6

Montoya JN (2001) La autoridad formal una restricción en las organizaciones. Una propuesta toc. I J Bus Financ Res. IBFR. Global. ISSN 1931-0277, ISSN 1931-0269, ISSN 1931-1285

Morgan G (1991) Imágenesdela Organización, pp 337–338. Alfaomega. México. Imágenes de las organizaciones, 408 p. Alfa Omega, Rama, México

Perrow C (1972) Why Bureaucracy. Ensayo publicado en Complex. Organizations Glenview, Scott, Foreman and Company. Glenview, IL

Perrow C (1998) Sociología de las organizaciones pp 317–318. Ed. McGraw Hill, Tercera edición, Madrid

Petit F (1984) Sicología de las Organizaciones. Herder, Barcelona, pp 17–40

Pfeffer J (1995) La Ecuación Humana: La Dirección de RH Clave para la Excelencia Empresarial

Senge P (1993) The fifth discipline, Doubleday Plub., New York (versión española La Quinta Disciplina, Granica, Barcelona. at. ol. (2000). La danza del cambio. 28. Editorial Norma, Santa Fé de Bogotá)

Shewart W (1939) Statistical method from the viewpoint of quality control. The Graduate School, The Department of Agriculture, Washington, p 155

Valle R, Martín F, Romero PM, Doland SL (2000) Business strategy work processes and human resource training: are they congruence? J Organ Behav, 21:283–297

Weber M (1895) El Estado nacional y la política económica. p. 29. En: Weber, Max. Obras selectas. (1953). Three types of ligitimate rule. pp 1–11 Berkley Journal of Sociology 4. (1964) Economía y sociedad. 227 FCE; México, México, cap. I, II y IV
Yin RK (1994) Case study research: design and methods. Sage Publications, Thousands Oaks
Zepeda Miramontes E (1997) Salarios relativos y región: el caso de la frontera norte de México. 124–152 Estudios Sociales: VII-4. México, septiembre-diciembre de 1997

A Study of the Human-Resource Practices and Challenges Confronted by Human-Resource Experts in an Indian IT Firm, Bangalore

Palaniappan Saravanan and Arumugam Vasumathi

Abstract The human-resource management function plays a critical role in partnering with business and external stakeholders and generates values and credibility to the organisation in terms of attaining their goals and objective for the organisation. The HR expert acts a change enabler by promoting change within the company. Changes within business functions must be addressed through guiding and generating policies and strategies to fulfill the business needs of the company. The HR function is anticipated to generate a value-enhanced amenity to the workers in order to meet upcoming business requirements. Major challenges occur due to increasing stress levels in the work environment. These issues that must be ameliorated through certain engagement initiatives systemetised by the employer and will have an impact manifested by lower attrition rates and the retaining of high-performers workers within the organisation. HR experts partner with business to counter various issues with respect to pre-onboarding requirements, formulating effective strategies and policies that address issues regarding employee performance and grievances, developing leadership skills, and retaining talented and high-performance workers, etc. This study helps identify and address the challenges confronted by HR experts during their day-to-day events at in Indian IT firm at Bangalore. The study determines that female employees are more satisfied with their job in its current role compared with male respondents.

Keywords Human-resource management · Change enabler · Performance engagement · Stress management · Strategic partner

---

P. Saravanan (✉) · A. Vasumathi
VIT University, Vellore, Tamil Nadu, India
e-mail: saravananec@gmail.com

A. Vasumathi
e-mail: avasumathi@vit.ac.in

E. Lau et al. (eds.), *Selected Papers from the Asia-Pacific Conference on Economics & Finance (APEF 2016)*, DOI 10.1007/978-981-10-3566-1_7

1 Introduction

HRM plays a wider role in an organisation. The concept of HRM was originated during the 1970 s during the Indian Industrial Revolution and is currently known as "personnel management." The personnel department takes care of administration, welfare activities, and employee relations. Due to the rapid growth of industrial sectors, the focus shifted from administrative and transactional functions to transformational activity as human-resource management. HRM plays a vital role in the growth and development of an organisation by managing employee issues, performance, and engagement factors in the organisation (Chatterjee 2006).

Personal management was promoted during 1931 based on the recommendations of the Royal Commission Report to appoint a welfare officer to take care of welfare activities for employees at the workplace. During the Industrial Revolution in India in 1948, the Factories Act of India was formed to protect employees in the work environment.

The scope of welfare officers was increased to include taking care of employees and administrative as well as dismissal procedures per the Factories Act guidelines as described by the government. The government of India also promoted human-resource management through establishing leading b-schools in India, such as Xavier School of Management and the Indian Institute of Personnel Management, to help companies overcome management issues. However, a strategic tie-up existed between the company and the institute to resolve issues related to trade unions, employee grievances, introducing modern techniques and principles to implement, and challenges in the work environment. HRM gained important in the organisation by helping to formulate and design a process to improve the efficiency and effectiveness of the organisation (Sucheta 2012).

HRM practices play an important role in improving company performance through formulating the necessary policies and strategies to improve the knowledge, skills, and attitudes of employees in the organisation (Colakoglu et al. 2006; Azmi 2011). The practices mainly focus on enhancing the services offered to customers, decreasing overhead costs, developing an engaged workforce, improving employee performance, controlling attrition, and decreasing stress in the workplace (Nishii et al. 2008).

HRM helps in identifying and bridging the gap between current performance and future organisation requirements through various training programs offered to employees, promoting leadership skills, increasing employee efficacy, and fulfilling employees' learning needs. HRM also helps in establishing a formal communication channel for better connections and aligning the organisational strategy with HR strategy to achieve better business outcomes (Nkhwangwa 2014).

1.1 Growth of the Indian IT Sector

The IT industry is projected to grow up to $300 billion by the year 2020, and the industry is expecting its growth to be up to 13–16% in the market. The industry mainly focuses on emerging technologies such as mobile computing, cloud computing, social networking, and cloud-based analytic systems. The industries maneuver from various parts of the country and tier 1 cities such as Chennai, Hyderabad, Mumbai, and Bangalore. Due to the increase in infrastructure and the resulting increased costs, companies are focusing on shifting their operations from tier 2 and tier 3 cities such as Mohali, Nagpur, Gurgaon, Mysore, Jaipur, Chandigarh, and Pune (KPMG and NSDC Report 2013).

Indian IT companies play an important role in developing the GDP ratio. In FY 2015–2016, industry is expected to grow to 130$ billion. The domestic sector is projected to grow to 10–12%, and >16,000 companies add 5–8% additional customers ever year, which contributes 10–12% of growth to GDP of the country. Bangalore is known as Silicon Valley of India: The city contributes up to 33% of software exports in India. Mumbai is known as the business capital of India; the majority of Indian companies have their headquarters in Mumbai. Few IT companies have started their operations from Kerala despite trade union issues; for example, TCS has its training center in Trivandrum. The company has invested approximately 10 billion INR and generated 10,000-person seating capacity in Trivandrum training center. The major verticals focused on by the industry are manufacturing, retail, oil and gas, banking, health care, financial services, e-commerce, telecom, and cloud computing, etc. (Taranjit and Batra 2014).

Indian IT companies gain an advantage in terms of outsourcing requirements from multinational companies due to the availability of a skilled workforce, high quality of service offered to customers, and cost-efficiency. India generates 2.3 million degree holders and 3,00,000 post-graduates across every year through 347 institutions all over the country (AON Report 2012).

The information-technology industry created a revolution in the Indian market by offering a cost-efficient communication platform, internet channels, and video-conferencing facilities, etc. The IT industry helps business to operate 24/7 around–the-clock service, which allows business to operate from various places in the country without any hindrance through the help of Internet technology. Internet technology plays an important role in web surfing, online shopping that allows delivering the product to the customer's doorstep, and staying connected with friends and family through various social-networking platforms, etc. (Kumar 2014).

1.2 Statement of the Problem

HR plays an important role in engaging the work force because employee engagement will result in improved employee productivity. An engaged work force will have a better connections, increased level of motivation, be able to accept more responsibilities at work, be energised, and aspire toward better work performance. Higher engagement levels will have a direct impact on company growth and its performance. Engaged employees focus on attaining organisational goals, formulating high-performance teams, building relationships between employees and the employer, and creating a better work environment (Priyadarshni 2016).

Motivation is a key factor that engages the work force to overcome challenges and creates confidence that helps in building strong relationship between employees and the employer (Katzell and Thompson 1990). By encouraging employees to be part of the decision-making process will help improve their performance and commitment toward the job and also acts as a retention tool in terms of retaining the best talent in the organisation (Haizlip 2008).

HR experts promote the change-management process through creating transparent communication channels, promoting a learning culture in the work environment, and facilitating change that improves the work climate (Agarwal 2008). The performance of an employee can be improved through offering employees a wide range of training opportunities within or outside of the organisation that will result in improving performance toward the current job (Blanchard and Witts 2009).

HR plays a crucial role in bridging the gap between personal and professional life through work–life balance initiative by formulating the necessary policies and strategies through various engagements that promote work–life balance initiatives such as flexible working hours, flexible working week, and extending the work-from-home policy, which also helps in managing both personal and professional life. All of these result in reducing the stress factors in the work environment and help in building confidence and integrity toward the work (Ellen et al. 2002). The HR manager should create policies and strategies that improve employee performance by maximum utilisation of available resources, investments in training individual capabilities, rewarding and encouraging a high-performance workforce through promoting rewards and recognition programs, and managing attrition levels through offering a wide range of career-development opportunities within the organisation (Vishva Prasad 2015).

By analysing various literature, the researchers determined that the issues faced with reference to job satisfaction, level of motivation, engagement levels, and work as well as personal life is completely different for IT industries compared with other industries in the country. HR experts face various issues due to factors such as employee satisfaction and motivation levels, engaging employees, and promoting work–life balance, all of which have a potential direct impact on stress levels in the workplace, employee-attrition levels, and employee attitudes toward the job. HR experts place an important role on engaging a talented workforce. By reading various literature reviews, it was identified that no study has previously been performed on the human-resource practices and challenges confronted by HR experts in an Indian IT firm. This motivated the researchers to conduct such a study.

2 Research Objectives

The objectives of the study were as follows:

- Identify the various human-resource practices and challenges confronted by HR experts in an Indian IT firm.
- Determine the relationship between gender and level of satisfaction toward the current job.
- Determine the association between years of experience and response toward employee engagement within the organisation.
- Determine the association between respondents' demographic profile and the work–life balance offered by the company.
- Predict the level of motivation given the respondents' demographic profile.

3 Literature Review

3.1 Employee Participation in the Decision-Making Process

HR plays a crucial role in developing employee participation in the decision-making process. The process helps managers identify and recognise the contribution of their employees at their work. Participation results in better decisions, generating a positive attitude among the workforce, and increasing the level of employee satisfaction with the job (Lawrence et al. 2014).

Employee participation leads to improved interpersonal skills and serves as a knowledge sharing forum. This practice results in implementing better decisions within the organisation (Davenport and Volpel 2001).

Employee involvement gains an important role in the industry, which results in implementing decisions more quickly, gaining financial and technology benefits, improving individual efficiency, building relationships between employees and the employer, and decreasing stress levels in the work environment, all of which have a impact on attrition levels at the organisation and gaining a competitive advantage in the industry (Shivangee Singh et al. 2011).

3.2 Creating a Motivational Workplace

HR professionals play a major role in creating a motivational work environment through offering incentive programs, fulfilling the short-term needs of the workers, and rewarding a talented workforce when organisational objectives are met. An increased motivation factor at work will result in increased employee productivity. A motivated workforce will express and deliver positive energy and attitude toward their work. The workforce is motivated through monetary and non-monetary terms such as rewards and recognition programs, cash incentives, paid leaves, travel allowance, bonus, cash-reward programs, etc. Recognising employees for their work will help to create a positive work environment and a better work climate. HR managers can help formulate a better work culture and work climate, which will help in developing the productivity level of workforce in the organisation (Vinay 2014).

Motivation plays a crucial factor during difficult times in terms of meeting challenging goals, generating a talented and engaged workforce at all levels, promoting confidence at work, increasing employee commitment, and increasing employee performance and motivational levels, all of which have a focus on realistic goals, which have a direct impact on employee productivity levels. This helps in obtaining the goals and objectives for the organisation (Fishbach et al. 2006).

Motivational factors will improve employees" confidence level, generate a talented workforce in the organisation, and motivate employees to take on challenging tasks that help in obtaining the company objectives, etc. (Koo and Fishbach 2008).

3.3 Leadership Engagement

Developing leadership skills will help create a talented workforce within the company. Leaders play an important role in guiding and motivating employees to get on the right path and setting clear, realistic goals for the company (Griffin and Parker 2010). Leadership skills focus on task-oriented processes, generates bonding between employee and the employer, enables a clear vision for the company, focuses on persuasive directions, and creates a strong communication channel for employees. There is a positive and strong relationship between employee performance and leadership skills. The employees with fewer motivation skills will have a lower degree of organisational performance (Hackman and Wageman 2005).

Leadership skills help to create a motivated workforce, improve employee performance, and creates employee growth factors. The leadership style will have a strong focus on improving the organisation's performance and achieving the desired business results (Fry 2003). Leadership factors promote individual performance and organisational growth through leadership engagement by identifying and developing future leaders in the organisation (Van Emmerik et al. 2010),

Leadership plays a major role in formulating and incorporating the necessary strategies to improve the skills required of employees. It also focuses on improving the knowledge, behavior, attitudes, interpersonal skills, motivational spirit, communication, focus, and customer-centric behavior of employees and also adds more value to business functions (Christman and McClellan 2012).

3.4 Retention Strategies

Retention is a key factor that controls attrition levels in the industry. An effective retention tool will result in obtaining better business outcomes. A committed workforce will help in increasing performance levels; improving employee work culture, attitude, and skills; and decreasing attrition rates. Improved work performance will result in a lower absenteeism rate, increased employee motivation, better connections with peers and subordinates, and a better and healthy work environment (Mita et al. 2014).

HR managers promote career-development engagements in order to retain talented resources in the organisation, prevent employees leaving the organisation due to improper communication, developing proper retention policies, and facilitation a proper mechanism to address grievances between the employer and supervisor. The employer should focus on developing a mechanism to address grievances, creating a stress-free work environment, and promoting a better work culture and climate, etc. (Bagga 2013).

HR should create a policies and necessary strategies to attract and retain talented employees by offering a wide range of learning opportunities, promoting self-development engagements, creating an improved feedback-based mechanism, facilitate open and transparent communication, organise coaching and mentoring programs, promote succession-planning programs to help employees climb the "corporate ladder," and have a plan to retain employees in the organisation (Kaliprasad 2006).

3.5 Work–Personal Life Balance

HR plays an important role in creating a balance between personal and work life through creating wide range of initiatives offered within the company. This will also result in decreasing employee turnover in the organisation and acts as a retention tool for the employer in order to gain a competitive advantage in the industry (Karatepe 2013).

Work–life balance can be obtained through generating a positive workforce and creating a positive work environment, improving job satisfaction, and increasing employees' commitment levels to stay in the organisation. Negative factors result in increased absenteeism, increased labour turnover, negative feeling toward work, etc. Formulating various policies related to flexible working hours, flexible working week, better recruitment practices, and learning initiatives will help in managing better the work culture and manage WLB among employees (Deery 2008).

HR managers should also focus on meeting the needs and requirements of employees that help create a balance between personal and professional life, which result in creating a better work climate, a transparent communication channel, and better training programs, which serve as the best retention tool for the organisation (Ans De Vos and Annelies Meganck 2009).

3.6 Workforce Planning

Workforce planning results in maximum utilisation of resources and identifying the right resources at the right places at right times. It is a process of identifying the gap between the existing resources and future requirements of an organisation. The planning process improves employees' performance through organising various training programs and learning initiatives within workplace and anticipating cost benefits with the maximum utilisation of resources with the minimum available resources (Deepa et al. 2013).

Workforce planning determines the following:

- Identifying the number of employees
- Retain a talented workforce
- Managing the existing available resources
- Developing and motivating employees to next level within the organisation

Manpower planning determines the present and future human requirements to meet the objectives of the organisation. The process creates a linkage between HRM practices and strategic requirements of the organisation. It is a process of identifying the company's demands and evaluating the available resources to meet those demands (Reilly 2003). The process determines the retention strategies and talent branding, decreases absenteeism, promotes job rotation, increases employee job satisfaction and motivation levels (Maina and Kwasira 2015).

Workforce planning plays an important role in the organisation because proper planning will result in achieving the company's goals and projecting the long-terms growth for the organisation. It requires the organisation to focus on the required competences to analyse the future needs of the company (Ghazala and Habib 2012). The process helps in identifying the necessary requirements at the recruitment stage and determines the workforce needs to the employer (Gupta 2008).

4 Model of Modern HR Practices

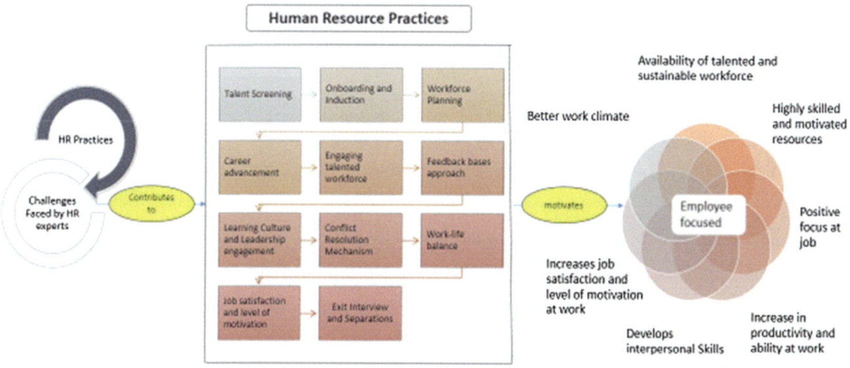

5 Research Methodology

5.1 *Type of Research*

The purpose of analysing the descriptive research is to study a phenomenon that occurs at particular place and time. Basis on the said factor, descriptive research was executed in this study.

5.2 *Sample*

The sample size defined as:

$$n = (z\sigma/d)2.$$

where n-sample size of the population.

z Value at a complete level of confidence.
σ Standard deviation of the population.
d Difference between the population mean and sample mean.

It is challenging to determine the standard deviation and population mean; hence, the researchers used a systematic sampling method, and the survey was conducted with HR experts at an Indian IT firm. The company operates from various parts of India such as Mysore, Mangalore, Trivandrum, Jaipur, Chandigarh,

Gurgaon, Bhubaneswar, Hyderabad, Pune, and Mumbai with 450 HR experts working from various development centers in India. In the Bangalore development center, approximately 150 h experts are employed in the firm. Hence, the researchers approached 75 HR experts, who were ready to respond for the primary data collection through questionnaire and considered as sample size for this study. This is the main limitation of the study.

5.3 Research Instrument

This study was purely empirical in nature; hence, a questionnaire was used as a sole instrument for data collection. The researchers framed a well-structured questionnaire consisting of three categories. The first category deals with the demographic profile of the HR experts; the second category deals with human-resource practices; and the third category contains various issues and challenges confronted by HR experts in the IT company. The researchers performs a validity test for the variables in the questionnaire in order to measure the human-resource practices and challenges encountered by HR experts (43 items with a Likert-type scale in the questionnaire) and obtained $\alpha = 0.7$. The questions were used for the validity test including respondents' responses toward their "level of satisfaction," "Work–life balance," "employee-engagement initiatives," "motivation levels," and "career engagements," etc.

5.4 Sources of Data

Primary source of data and information collected through questionnaires and the secondary source of data were journals, publications, books, and the handbook of the IT firm.

5.5 Data-Analysis Procedures

The primary information collected through questionnaires and their responses were keyed in and analysed using SPSS (Statistical Package for Social Sciences) for analysis. Pearson's Chi-Square was used to identify whether two random variables were independent in nature. Hence, the researchers were able to determine the significant level of association between years of experience and response toward employee engagement at the organisation. Correlation analysis was used to identify the degree of relationship between the dependent and independent variables. Hence, the researchers were able to determine the relationship between gender and level of satisfaction toward the current job.

Discriminant analysis identified the association between one dependent variable (dichotomous questionnaire) and many independent variables. Hence, discriminant analysis revealed the significant association between work–life balance engagements with gender, age, annual income, educational qualification, and years of experience in the organisation. Multiple regression was helpful to find out the important independent variables among all other independent variables to predict the dependent variable. Therefore, multiple regression analysis was performed to determine the HR experts' level of motivation toward the work with gender, age, educational qualification, annual income, and years of experience. The investigators determined that employee number of years of experience is a more important independent variable than other variables in predicting the level of employee motivation factors toward their work faced by HR experts.

6 Findings and Data Analysis

6.1 *Correlation Analysis*

Relationship between gender and level of satisfaction toward the current job.

The Pearson's correlation value (Table 1) was 0.049, which revealed that there is a positive correlation between gender and level of satisfaction toward the current job. Most of the female respondents are satisfied with their job toward the current role compared with male respondents.

6.2 *Chi-Square*

Hypothesis no. 1: There is a significant association between years of experience and response regarding employee engagement at the organisation.

The Chi-square presents a significance level of 0.469 at the 95% confidence level (Table 2). This number is greater than the hypothetical value of 0.05. Hence,

Table 1 Correlation value

Particulars		Value	Asymptomatic SE	Approximate *T*	Approximate *p*
Interval by interval	Pearson's R	0.049	0.116	0.415	0.679
Ordinal by ordinal	Spearman correlation	0.034	0.119	0.293	0.770
No. of valid cases	75				

Table 2 Chi-square

Particulars	Value	Approximate significance
Nominal by nominal	0.340	0.469
Phi	0.196	0.469
No. of valid cases	75	

Table 3 Symmetric measures

Particulars	Value	df	Asymptomatic p (2-sided)
Pearson Chi-Square	8.660	9	0.469
Likelihood ratio	8.918	9	0.445
Linear-by-linear association	0.820	1	0.365
No. of valid cases	75		

hypothesis no. 1 is accepted: There is a significant association between years of experience and response toward employee engagement at the organisation.

Cramer's V is 0.469 (Table 3), which reveals that there is a moderate association between years of experience and response regarding employee engagement at the organisation.

The asymmetric-lambda value is 0.000 (Table 4), which reveals that there is a 0% error reduction in predicting responses regarding years of experience and those regarding employee engagement at the organisation. If the lambda value increases then dependent variable output could be predictable. Hence, the researchers could predict responses regarding years of experience and as well as those regarding employee engagement at the organisation. Here the researchers cannot determine participants' response regarding years of experience nor those regarding employee engagement at the organisation.

6.3 *Discriminant Analysis*

Hypothesis no. 2: There is a significant association between gender, age, educational qualification, annual income, and years of experience with work–life balance at the company (Tables 5, 6, 7 and 8).

The classification matrix (Table 9) indicates that the discriminant functions were able to classify 69.3% of the 75 objects correctly. The Wilks' lambda value (Table 3) is 0.852. The value falls between 0 and 1, which indicates the better discriminating power of the variables selected. The probability value of the F-test determined that the discrimination between the two groups is extremely significant. Because $p < 0.107$, it indicates the F-test would be significant at a confidence level up to $(1 - 0.045) \times 100$ or 95.5%. Hence, hypothesis no. 2 is accepted.

The standardised coefficient (Table 4) reveals that gender is the best predictor with a coefficient of 0.757 followed by age (coefficient = 0.564), annual income (coefficient = 0.491), educational qualification (coefficient = –0.520, and years of experience

Table 4 Directional measures

Particulars			Value	Asymptomatic SE	Approximate T	Approximate significance
Nominal by nominal	Asymmetric lambda		0.038	0.047	0.778	0.437
		Employee-engagement dependent	0.000	0.000		
		Years of experience–dependent	0.067	0.083	0.778	0.437
	Goodman and Kruskal tau	Employee engagement	0.019	0.014		0.903
		Years of experience–dependent	0.040	0.027		0.439

Table 5 Wilks' lamba

Test of function (s)	Wilks' lamda	Chi-square	df	*p*
1	0.953	3.414	5	.045

Table 6 Standardised canonical discriminant-function coefficients

Particulars	Function
	1
Gender	0.757
Age	0.564
Education qualification	−0.520
Annual income	0.491
Years of experience	−0.979

Table 7 Canonical discriminant-function coefficients

Particulars	Function
	1
Gender	1.559
Age	0.698
Education qualification	−0.801
Annual income	0.443
Years of experience	−1.169
(Constant)	−0.566

Unstandardised coefficients

Table 8 Functions at group centroids

Work–life balance	Function
	1
No	−0.257
Yes	0.660

Unstandardised canonical discriminant functions were evaluated at group means

Table 9 Classification results

Details		Work–life balance	Predicted group membership		Total
			Yes	No	
Original	Count	Yes	35	19	54
		No	4	17	21
	%	Yes	64.8	35.2	100.0
		No	19.0	81.0	100.0

Of the original grouped cases, 69.3% were correctly classified (coefficient –0.979.6). The means of the canonical variables (Table 6) shares the new means for the transformed group centroids. Hence, the new mean for group 1 (non-work–life balance) is –0.257, and the new mean for group 2 (work–life balance) is 0.660. This means that the midpoint of these two is 0. This is clear when the two means are plotted on a straight line and their midpoints are located as shown below.

Chart 1		
−0.257	0	0.660
Mean for group 1 (no work–life balance)		Mean for group 2 (work–life balance)

If the discriminant scores of a respondent falls left of the mid points, this infers that the respondents rated positively the work–life balance offered in the company; if a respondent's score is falls right of the midpoint, the respondent rated that no work–life balance is offered by the company. Therefore, any positive (> 0) value of the discriminant score will lead to classification the career-development opportunities *are* offered within the company, and any negative (< 0) value of the discriminant score will lead to classification there is no work–life balance in the organisation.

Unstandardised discriminant function (Table 7) is

$$Y = -0.566 + 1.559\,(\text{gender}) + 0.698\,(\text{age}) - 0.801\,(\text{educational qualification}) + 0.443\,(\text{annual income}) - 1.169\,(\text{years of experience}).$$

Y gives discriminant scores of any person based on the categories of gender, age, educational qualification, annual income, and years of experience.

For example, a female HR professional in the age group 40 years who completed her post-graduate degree and who currently has experience >12 years falls under the category of annual income >7 lakhs provided that there is work–life balance in the organisation. This can be proven by the following equation.

The researches coded in SPSS were as follows: A female HR professional respondent (coded in SPSS as 2), falls under age group of 40 yrs (4), education qualification as post-graduate (3), annual income >7 Lakhs (4), with >12 years of experience (4). By calculating these values into the above said discriminant function, the discriminant score *Y* is as follows:

$$\begin{aligned} \mathrm{Y} &= -0.566 + 1.559\,(\text{gender}) + 0.698\,(\text{age}) \\ &\quad - 0.801\,(\text{educational qualification}) + 0.443\,(\text{annual income}) \\ &\quad - 1.169\,(\text{years of experience}). \\ \mathrm{Y} &= -0.566 + 1.559(2) + 0.698(4) - 0.801(3) + 0.443(4) - 1.169(4). \\ \mathrm{Y} &= -0.566 + 3.118 + 2.792 - 2.403 + 1.772 - 4.676. \\ \mathrm{Y} &= 0.037. \end{aligned}$$

From chart 1, the preceding Y-value of 0.037 shows the decision rule of the discriminant score left of the midpoint 0, which leads to a classification of work–life balance available in the organisation.

6.4 Regression Analysis

Factors identifying the relationship between level of motivation at work and the respondents are age, gender, qualification gained, annual income, and years of experience through regression analysis (Tables 10, 11 and 12).

In the output of the regression model, the value of B gives all the coefficients of the model, which are as follows:

$$\begin{aligned} \mathrm{Y} = {} & 2.293 + 0.337\,(\text{gender}) - 0.029\,(\text{age}) - 0.118\,(\text{education qualification}) \\ & + 0.188\,(\text{annual income}) - 0.360\,(\text{years of experience}). \end{aligned}$$

From the above equation, it can be inferred that the female employees are highly motivated toward the job and the best predictor variable is gender with a higher coefficient of 0.337. The factors of age, educational qualification, and years of

Table 10 Model summary

Model	R	R^2	Adjusted R^2	SE of the estimate
1	0.300	0.090	0.024	1.123

Table 11 Analysis of variance

Model	Sum of squares	df	Mean square	F	Significance
1 Regression	8.613	5	1.723	1.365	0.248
Residual	87.067	69	1.262		
Total	95.680	74			

Table 12 Coefficients

Model	Unstandardised coefficients		Standardised coefficient	T	p
	B	SE	Beta		
1 (constant)	2.293	0.732		3.132	0.003
Gender	0.337	0.269	0.149	1.254	0.214
Age	−0.029	0.228	−0.021	−0.129	0.898
Education qualification	−0.118	0.253	−0.067	−0.465	0.643
Annual income	0.188	0.159	0.183	1.186	0.240
Years of experience	–0.360	0.211	–0.270	–1.706	0.093

experience have a negative coefficient, and those of gender and annual income have a positive coefficient, which shows a statistically significant *t*-value of 0.898.

The *p*-level is observed to be 0.248, indicating that the model is statistically significant. The R^2 value is 0.090. The Student *t*-test for significance of an individual dependent variable indicates that at the significance level of 0.05 (confidence level of 95%), only gender is statistically significant in the model. Experienced female HR experts are highly motivated toward their job compared with other factors such as age, years of experience, annual income, and education qualification.

6.4.1 Forward Regression

Given an output of forward regression, the regression ends up with one of five independent variables remaining in the regression model. The variable "years of experience" is statistically significant at the 95% confidence level. The *F*-test of the model is also highly significant, and the R^2 value is 0.053 (Tables 13, 14, 15 and 16).

$$Y = 2.844 - 0.306 \text{ (years of experience)}.$$

6.4.2 Backward Regression Analysis

The results of the backward regression analysis show that only "years of experience" remains in the model to predict the effectiveness level of motivation at work

Table 13 Model summary

Model	*R*	R^2	Adjusted^2	SE of the estimate
1	0.230	0.053	0.040	1.114

Table 14 Analysis of variance

Model	Sum of squares	df	Mean square	*F*	*p*
1 Regression	5.059	1	5.059	4.075	0.047
Residual	90.621	73	1.241		
Total	95.680	74			

Table 15 Coefficients

Model	Unstandardised coefficients		Standardised coefficient	*T*	*p*
	B	SE	Beta		
1 (constant)	2.844	0.326		8.730	0.000
Years of experience	−0.306	0.152	−0.230	−2.019	0.047

compared with other independent variables. The independent variables are statistically significant at the 95% confidence level. The F-test of the model is also highly significant, and the R^2 value is 0.053 (Tables 17, 18, 19 and 20).

$$Y = 2.844 - 0.306 \text{ (years of experience)}.$$

Table 16 Excluded variables

Model	Beta In	T	p	Partial correlation	Collinearity statistics
					Tolerance
1 Gender	0.137	1.196	0.236	0.140	0.976
Age	– 0.029	– 0.199	0.843	−0.023	0.605
Educational qualification	0.15	0.128	0.898	0.015	0.959
Annual income	0.129	0.985	0.328	0.115	0.756

Table 17 Model summary

Model	R	R^2	Adjusted R^2	SE of the estimate
1	0.300	0.090	0.024	1.123
2	0.300	0.090	0.038	1.115
3	0.293	0.086	0.047	1.110
4	0.267	0.071	0.046	1.111
5	0.230	0.053	0.040	1.114

Table 18 Analysis of variance

Model	Sum of squares	df	Mean square	F	p
1 Regression	8.613	5	1.723	1.365	0.248
Residual	87.067	69	1.262		
Total	95.680	74			
2 Regression	8.592	4	2.148	1.727	0.154
Residual	87.088	70	1.244		
Total	95.680	74			
3 Regression	8.232	3	2.744	2.228	0.092
Residual	87.448	71	1.232		
Total	95.680	74			
4 Regression	6.823	2	3.412	2.764	0.070
Residual	88.857	72	1.234		
Total	95.680	74			
5 Regression	5.059	1	5.059	4.075	0.047
Residual	90.621	73	1.241		
Total	95.6807	74			

Table 19 Coefficients

Model	Unstandardised coefficients	Standardised coefficient		*T*	*p*
	B	SE	Beta		
1 (Constant)	2.293	0.732		3.132	0.003
Gender	0.337	0.269	0.149	1.254	0.214
Age	−0.029	0.228	−0.021	−0.129	0.898
Educational qualification	−0.118	0.253	−0.067	−0.465	0.643
Annual income	0.188	0.159	0.183	1.186	0.240
Years of experience	−0.360	0.211	−0.270	−1.706	0.093
2 (Constant)	2.285	0.724		3.155	0.002
Gender	0.342	0.263	0.151	1.300	0.198
Educational qualification	−0.128	0.238	−0.073	−0.539	0.592
Annual income	0.187	0.158	0.182	1.190	0.238
Years of experience	−0.375	0.176	−0.281	−2.130	0.037
3 (Constant)	2.067	0.598		3.458	0.001
Gender	0.330	0.261	0.146	1.264	0.210
Annual income	0.144	0.135	0.140	1.069	0.289
Educational qualification	−0.368	0.175	−0.276	−2.107	0.039
4 (Constant)	2.306	0.555		4.153	0.000
Gender	0.312	0.261	0.137	1.196	0.236
Years of experience	−0.278	0.153	−0.209	−1.815	0.074
5 (Constant)	2.844	0.326		8.730	0.000
Years of experience	−0.306	0.152	−0.220	−2.019	0.047

7 Findings and Conclusion

Based on the research and survey conducted in a group of HR experts, there is a positive correlation between gender and level of satisfaction with the current job. Most of the female respondents are satisfied with their job regarding their current role compared with male respondents. This finding aligns with the findings of Ogundele (2005), but it contradicts the findings of Kim (2005). From the analysis, it is proven that there is a significant association between years of experience and response regarding employee engagement at the organisation. This finding aligns with the findings of Sagayarani (2015) and those of Fatma and Shyqyri (2015), but contradicts with the findings of Elizabeth and Dennis (2014). From discriminant analysis, the researchers determined that there is a significant association between work–life balance initiatives organised by the company and gender, age, annual income, educational qualification, and years of experience. Of many independent variable, gender acts as important independent variable with higher a coefficient value, which predicts work–life balance engagements in the company compared

Table 20 Excluded variables

Model	Beta In	T	*p*	Partial correlation	Collinearity statistics
					Tolerance
2 Age	−0.021	−0.129	0.898	−0.015	0.504
3 Age	−0.045	−0.295	0.940	−0.035	0.562
Educational qualification	−0.073	−0.539	0.809	−0.064	0.708
4 Age	−0.006	−0.040	0.968	−0.005	0.594
Educational qualification	0.009	0.079	0.937	0.009	0.957
Annual income	0.140	1.069	0.289	0.126	0.753
5 Age	−0.029	−0.199	0.843	−0.023	0.605
Educational qualification	0.015	0.128	0.898	0.015	0.959
Annual income	0.129	0.985	0.328	0.115	0.756
Gender	0.137	1.196	0.236	0.140	0.976

with other independent variables. This result aligns with the findings of Amy et Al. (2014) but contradicts with the findings of Karishma and Harvinder (2015). Multiple regression analysis reveals that independent variables—such as age, gender, education qualification, annual income, and years of experience—are statistically significant with level of motivation at work. The study found that gender is the best predictor and gain importance in level of motivation at work. This finding aligns with the findings of Fapohunda (2014), but it contradicts with the findings of Rashmi et al. (2010).

8 Implications of the Study

HR experts act as a business-driven HR by incorporating necessary policies and practices with reference to onboarding and induction, manpower planning–induction process, and feedback-based system. The study also identifies and encourages a learning culture, leadership engagements, career advancements, employee-engagement drives, increasing the level of satisfaction, and work–life balance initiatives, etc. HR experts should focusing on and decrease attrition levels through a wide range of rewards and recognition programs, counseling, mentoring programs, creation of a positive and friendly work environment, promoting employment involvement, participation, and generating and retaining talented workforce in the organisation. This research helps to determine human-resource practice and the challenges confronted by HR experts in an Indian IT firm. The study is limited to an IT firm in Bangalore, India, but the results can be extrapolated to IT firms and other industries in India and abroad to get a better understanding of human-resource practices and the challenges faced by HR experts.

References

Agarwal A (2008) Employee motivation. http://ezinearticles.com. Accessed 25 Nov 2009

Amy W, Maria V, Renee F, Trish D (2014) Worklife balance satisfaction: an analysis of gender differences and contributing factors. NY J Stud Aff 14(2):1–25

Aon Report (2012) Industry analysis: IT consulting and services, http://www.advisenltd.com/wp-content/uploads/information-technology-industry-report-2012-12.pdf?bcsi_scan_ee7e30f120188340=0&bcsi_scan_filename=information-technology-industry-report-2012-12.pdf. Accessed 03 May 2016

Azmi FT (2011) Strategic human resource management and its linkage with HRM effectiveness and organizational performance: evidence from India. Int J Human Resour Manage 22(18):3888–3912

Bagga G (2013) How to keep the talent you have got. Human Resour Manage Int Digest 21(1):3–4

Blanchard S, Witts D (2009) Best practices in employee motivation. http://www.buzzle.com. Accessed 29 Dec 2009

Chatterjee SR, Coffey J (2006) Perspectives of human resource management in the Asia Pacific. Pearson Prentice Hall, Malaysia, pp 41–62

Christman DE, McClellan RL (2012) Discovering middle space: distinctions of sex and gender in resilient leadership. J High Educ 83(5):648–670

Colakoglu S, Lepak DP, Hong Y (2006) Measuring HRM effectiveness: considering multiple stakeholders in a global context. Human Resour Manage Rev 16(2):209–218

Davenport TH, Volpel SC (2001) The rise of knowledge towards attention management. J Knowl Manage 5(3):212–222

De Vos A, Meganck A (2009) What HR managers do versus what employees value. Person Rev 38(1):45–60

Deepa E, Kuppusamy S, Kamaleswari P (2013) Man power planning in retail sector: an empirical evaluation. Int J Market Financial Serv Manage Res 2(7):125–137

Deery M (2008) Talent management, work-life balance and retention strategies. Int J Contemp Hosp Manage 20(7):792–806

Elizabeth M, Dennis J (2014) Contingent rewards as a strategy for infiuencing employee engagement in manufacturing companies: case study of Williamson tea Kenya limited. Int J Bus Commer 4(5):20–59

Ellen A, Troy R, Elisa G (2002) Tales from the hiring line: effects of the internet and technology on HR processess. Org Dyn 31(3):224–244

Fapohunda M (2014) Gender infiuences in worklife balance: findings from Nigeria. Global J Human Resour Manage 2(2):25–39

Fatma J, Shyqyri L (2015) The impact of communication satisfaction and demographic variables on employee engagement. J Serv Sci Manage 1(8):191–200

Fishbach A, Dhar R, Zhang Y (2006) Subgoals as substitutes or complements: the role of goal accessibility. J Pers Soc Psychol 91(2):232–242

Fry LW (2003) Towards a theory of spiritual leadership. Leadersh Q 14(1):693–727

Ghazala I, Habib J (2012) J Bus Manage 3(6):06–13

Griffin MA, Parker SK, Mason CM (2010) Leader vision and the development of adaptive and proactive performance: alongitudinal study. J Appl Psychol 95(1):174–182

Gupta C (2008). Human resource management, 5th edn. Sultan Chand and Sons Educational Publishers, New Delhi, pp 3–5

Hackman JR, Wageman R (2005) A theory of team coaching. Acad Manag Rev 30(2):269–287

Haizlip T (2008) Employee motivation—10 tips to boost job performance. http://www.wzinearticles.com. Accessed 24 Oct 2009

Kaliprasad M (2006) The human factor 1: attracting, retaining, and motivating capable people. Cost Eng 48(6):20–26

Karatepe OM (2013) High-performance work practices, work social support and their effects on job embeddedness and turnover intentions. Int J Contemp Hospitality Manage 25(6):903–921

Karishma B, Harvinder S (2015) Impact of gender, satisfaction towards work life balance. J Bus Manage 17(3):48–53
Katzell RA, Thompson DE (1990) Work motivation: theory and practice. Am Psychol 45(1):144–153
Kim S (2005) Gender differences in the satisfaction of public workers: a study of Seoul Metropolitan Government, Korea. J Res Sex Roles 1(1):140–224
Koo M, Fishbach A (2008) Dynamics of self-regulation: how (un) accomplished goal actions affect motivation. J Pers Soc Psychol 94(2):183–195
Kumar P (2014) Information technology: roles, advantages and disadvantages. Int J Adv Res Comput Sci Softw Eng 4(6):1020–1024
Lawrence W et al (2014) Effect of employee participation in decision making on the organizational commitment amongst academic staff in the private and public universities in Kenya. Int J Adv Res Manage Social Sci 3(12):131–142
Maina DK, Kwasira J (2015) Role of human resource planning practices on employee performance in county governments in Kenya: a case of Nakuru county. Int J Econ Commer Manage 3 (5):1569–1580
Mita M, Aarti K, Ravneet D (2014) Study on employee retention and commitment. Int J Adv Res Comput Sci Manage Stud 2(2):154–164
Nishii LH, Lepak DP, Schneider B (2008) Employee attributions of the why of HR practices: their effects on employee attitudes and behaviors, and customer satisfaction. Pers Psychol 61 (3):503–545
Nkhwangwa LCT (2014) Achieving strategic fit/integration between business strategies and human resource management (HRM) strategies in the banking sector: an assessment of the commercial banks in Malawi. Int J Social Sci Manage 1(4):143–159
KPMG & NSDC Report (2013) http://www.nsdcindia.org/sites/default/files/files/hp-sg-report.pdf. Accessed 03 May 2016
Ogundele OJK (2005) Management and organisation: theory and behaviour. Molofin Nominee, Lagos
Priyadarshni N (2016) To study the impact of employee engagement on employee productivity and motivational level of employee in retail sector. IOSR J Bus Manage 1(1):41–47
Rashmi K, Cas K, Olle ten C, Gerda C (2010) Advance in health science education, effects of age, gender and educational background on strength of motivation for medical school. 15(1):303–313
Sagayarani A (2015) A study on employee engagement at pump industry. Int J Bus Manage 3 (4):257–265
Shivangee S et al (2011) Employee involvement. Int J Bus Manage Res 1(8):203–215
Sucheta M (2012) Unique HR practices in the Indian IT industry. Delhi Bus Rev 13(1):49–65
Taranjit S, Batra GS (2014) Information technology and it enabled services industry in India. Int J Comput Corp Res 4(1):1–18
Van Emmerik H, Wendt H, Euwema MC (2010) Gender ratio, societal culture, and male and female leadership. J Occup Organ Psychol 83(4):895–914
Vinay C (2014) Motivation in the workplace to improve the employee performance. Int J Eng Technol Manage Appl Sci 2(6):221–230
Vishva Prasad C (2015) Emerging trends in HRM. Int J Econ Res 12(2):1–8

Current Issues of the Labor Market in the Slovak Republic with an Emphasis on the Trends in Migration Policy

Eva Rievajova and Andrej Privara

Abstract The financial and economic crisis had very negative impacts on the Slovak labour market. Adverse effects of the crisis mainly affected the category of disadvantaged persons. A persistent problem is, however, also structural and regional unemployment. Trends in the Slovak labour market are also influenced by the migration of Slovaks for work abroad. On one hand, this helps to reduce the unemployment rate. In contrast, it has many disadvantages: mostly the labour shortage in some sectors and professions. Slovak migration policy should focus primarily on those sectors that are the most affected by labour migration (in particular the health sector).

Keywords Labour market · Employment · Migration policy · Highly qualified migrants

1 Introduction

The labor market is a sensitive and vulnerable sector of the Slovak economy. The recent years of the crisis in Slovakia since 2009 has taken a significant toll compared with most EU economies, which resulted in deepening structural problems in

This contribution is an output of VEGA project no. 1/0001/16 "Present and prospects of changes in employment and related processes in the context of achieving the objectives of the European Employment Strategy."

E. Rievajova (✉) · A. Privara
Faculty of National Economy, Department of Social Development,
University of Economics in Bratislava, Dolnozemska Cesta 1,
852 35 Bratislava, Slovak Republic
e-mail: eva.rievajova@euba.sk

A. Privara
e-mail: andy.privara@gmail.com

E. Lau et al. (eds.), *Selected Papers from the Asia-Pacific Conference on Economics & Finance (APEF 2016)*, DOI 10.1007/978-981-10-3566-1_8

the labor market and increasing the unemployment rate. The latest economic forecasts confirm that in Slovakia there an ongoing recovery in the context of low energy prices and a very accommodating monetary policy. Nevertheless, the labor market is still affected by the persistence of large regional disparities in economic growth and employment. As the European Commission states, unemployment remains one of the biggest problems of economic policy, also in relation to its structural characteristics.

Science and research, innovation, information technology, and especially young educated people are one of the priorities of every country. For these reasons, research on "brain drain" belongs in the category of very current and important economic problems in the twenty first century, although the last economic and financial crisis had for its impact a decrease in the flows of highly qualified labor.

2 Literature Review

High unemployment in the majority of the EU countries is related to low economic growth or its decrease as one of the consequences of the crisis after 2008. Recent trends in the labor market are a result partially of cyclical movements and particularly of deep economic crisis, but they are also caused also by structural and institutional problems of the labor market affecting the economic activity and the labor market performance. In the past 3 years, after the strongest consequences of the crisis faded away, Slovakia has made considerable efforts in eliminating the macroeconomic imbalances of the recent years. However, many problems still exist, and new challenges are emerging (Rievajova et al. 2015).

After the crisis, Slovakia had the highest economic growth among all EU countries and the convergence continues albeit at a slower pace. Economic production recovered, and in 2011 it reached the pre-crisis level, although the economic growth is lower than the one before the beginning of the crisis. The annual real GDP growth between the years 2012 and 2014 decreased to 1.8% on average, whereas for the period from 2006 to 2008 it was at an average of 8.3%. economic growth in the last quarter of 2015 was on the level of 4.3%, which was the best result in the last 5 years. Despite the continuing economic recovery, the output gap remained negative in 2015, and it is expected to close not sooner than 2017. The real convergence toward the developed EU member states still continues, but it does so slower than before the crisis. The Slovak real per-capita GDP in 2014 was approximately 75% of the EU average. The real GDP growth increased to 3.5% in 2015. The driving factor was a significant increase in the investment activity connected with the drawing of EU funds coupled a significant increase in household consumption (Europska komisia 2016).

It is expected that in coming years, the strongest stimulus for growth will be an increasing private consumption with a contribution of employment growth, real-wage growth, low credit costs, and a continuing decrease in energy prices.

However, some risks can emerge due to loss of exports, mainly in the automotive industry, what can be triggered, in particular, by external factors.

The economic slump of 2008 caused serious problems in Slovakia, and some signals of recovery in the labor market did not begin to show up until 2014, although some economic recovery was seen already in 2011. This development confirms again only tiny links between employment and economic growth, which are largely associated with long-term structural problems in the labor market (Lubyova et al. 2015, p. 18).

Trends in the Slovak labor market are influenced by the migration of Slovaks for work abroad. On one hand, this situation helps to decrease the unemployment rate. In contrast, it has also its disadvantages: Some sectors and professions start to suffer from a shortage of workforce. Moreover, we have observed a negative trend in the structure of Slovak emigrants since the late 1990s: The ratio of highly educated workers leaving our homeland is increasing.

Regarding the emigration of highly qualified workers from the Slovak Republic and its effect on society, some experts estimate the number of graduates each year leaving from Slovakia to be from 7 to 10,000 people, which represents from one fourth to one third of all university graduates, which is a much higher proportion than in neighboring countries. This has, among other effects, resulted in weaker GDP growth and a slower increase in the educational level of the population. Brain drain from the Slovak Republic affects its general economic development (Divinsky 2014). Individual authors point out the ambiguous effect on the Slovak economy and society. On one hand, they notice a significant amount of remittances that emigrants send or bring home. In contrast, they point out the negative consequences in the social arena arising from the radical limitation of contacts with friends, colleagues, and the local community (USZZ 2008). Significant negative effects are also related to difficulties faced by immigrants in terms of their social and economic reintegration when they return home.

Seeing that students are a kind of precursor of highly qualified migrants, the issue of the development trends of Slovak citizens studying abroad became an integral part of the study of the brain drain. In this regard, we note that Slovakia recorded since 1998 an unprecedented increase of the proportion of its students abroad. According to OECD data, this number more than quadrupled in the period 1998–2012 (from 3400 to 36,200). This increase is related to the continuously increasing share of students studying in the Czech Republic (Bahna 2015). According to OECD data, 15% of Slovak university students studied abroad in 2012. Among the OECD countries, a higher percentage of their students at foreign universities involved only two countries: Iceland and Luxembourg.

Empirical studies dealing with the emigration of highly educated people from Slovakia consider the main reasons for this phenomenon to be the quality of grants in science and research, level and methods of organizing a scientific research, transparency in awarding research grants, career opportunities for young scientists, and equipment available at the research institutions (Kostelecka and Bernard 2007).

3 Research Objective

The aim of this analysis was to identify and evaluate the development of the labor market in the Slovak Republic with an emphasis on unemployment. We analysed the causes of changes in the structure of emigrants from the Slovak Republic occurring since the late 90s. Our analysis lead to the formulation of some recommendations oriented to decrease brain drain from Slovakia.

4 Key Results

The high unemployment rate in Slovakia is one of the most serious economic and social problems which has avoided for a long time full realization of the growth potential of the Slovak economy. The last highest growth in the unemployment rate linked with a decrease in employment was reflected in an economic slump due to the global crisis in 2010, when almost one in six individuals in the active population was seeking a job, and the average annual unemployment rate was 14%. During the next 4 years, the share of economically active people seeking a job was >13%. Neighbouring countries from the Visegrad Group did much better, Hungary had the closest evolution of its unemployment rate to the Slovak one 2–3 percentage points fewer compared with Slovakia, and the Czech Republic recorded a post-crisis unemployment rate 5–6 percentage points lower compared with the Slovak one (Lubyova et al. 2015, p. 17) (Graph 1).

As stated in the Country Report for 2016 (Europska komisia 2016), structural unemployment, reflecting high geographical disparities, remains a key political problem. Significant geographical differences in the labor market, multiplied by the low mobility of the workforce, contribute to the fact that the country has one of the highest long-term unemployment rates in the EU. Results of the Slovak labor market still cannot be considered as satisfactory. Although the employment rate is relatively low, and unemployment rate is high, some social groups—such as low-qualified workers, young workers, marginalized Roma people, and mothers with young children—are particularly vulnerable. Unemployment is also

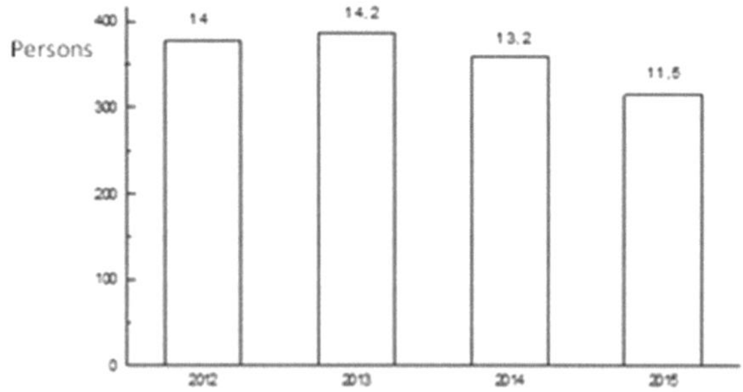

Graph 1 Unemployment (in thousands and %). *Source* Statistical Office of the Slovak Republic, own processing

concentrated in the center and eastern parts of the country. Low sensitivity of unemployment to increases of real wages only underlines the concerns about the size of the structural unemployment.

Unemployment is often a long-term issue. Slovakia belongs to the group of countries that fight a particularly high and long-term unemployment rate. This phenomenon contributes significantly to negative developments of the public finances, but it also reflects the insufficient use of production capacities in the economy. The high unemployment rate is not associated only with a lack of demand for labor but also with the result of disharmony between them (Tiruneh et al. 2014). In 2014, the rate of long-term unemployment rate (>12 months) was one of the highest in the EU (9.3% vs. 5.1% in the EU-28). Among unemployed people, two thirds belong to the group of long-term unemployed; the majority of the long-term unemployed did not have work for >2 years; and the rate of very long-term unemployment is 6.6% (more than twice the EU average). Long-lasting unemployment is a significant risk for low-skilled workers and young people. Slovakia has the highest unemployment rate for workers (age 20–64 years) with low qualifications in the EU (36.9% vs. 16.3% in the EU-28 in the third quarter of 2015). Low-qualified workers also represent a high percentage of long-term unemployed people. In 2014, low-skilled workers represented 24% of long-term unemployed compared with 4% of low-skilled workers among the employed population (Graph 2).

Regional disparities in unemployment are still considerable. In 2014, the unemployment rate in Bratislava was still >2 times lower than in Eastern Slovakia (6.0% vs. 16.6%, respectively) despite some progress being made in the elimination of these differences. The main reasons for these differences can be explained by a combination of low growth and weak capacity to create jobs in the central and eastern parts of the country as well as insufficient regional labor mobility to the parts of the country with a greater number of job vacancies. The factors contributing to a lack of greater mobility are an insufficient transport infrastructure, high travel

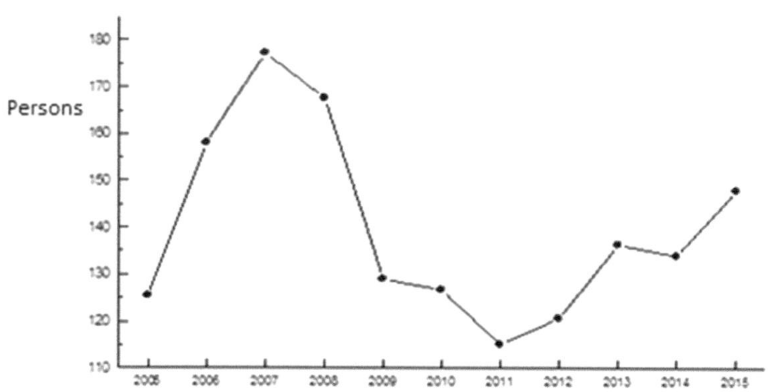

Graph 2 Number of Slovaks working abroad (in thousands). *Source* Statistical Office of the Slovak Republic, own processing

and accommodation costs compared with the average wage, and an underdeveloped market of rental accommodation.

In 2015, Slovakia adopted a law for supporting the regions with a high unemployment rate based on existing policies related to investment support, social housing, and infrastructure development. In order to promote internal mobility of the workforce, Slovakia changed the requirements for "relocation allowance" for unemployed people who find a job at least 70 km from their domicile.

According to the OECD statistics, Slovakia is gaining on the leaders of economic migration. Compared with other developed countries, Slovakia holds the ninth place among all OECD countries with the highest work emigration for work abroad. The number of Slovaks working abroad has increased from 130,000 to 148,000 in the last 3 years. Many Slovaks left Slovakia for working abroad during the pre-crisis years of 2006–2008, so the decline occurred after the beginning of the global crisis that affected the host countries as well. In the recent years, after the economic recovery, the trend increased again. This fact is also one of the indicators of decreased unemployment rate and increased employment rate. Most of the Slovaks who left the country now work in the Czech Republic and Austria mainly due to higher wages.

Scientists who study international migration in the Slovak Republic encounter a problem of a lack of quality information. They must suffice only with existing estimates. According to them, approximately one quarter of our university graduates leave Slovakia every year to work abroad. As stated by Bleha and Vaňo (2007), although the quantitative level does not confirm a predicted high number of working emigrants after the Slovakia's accession to the European Union, an important fact is that it is a population in the age range of the highest fertility, which negatively influences the age structure of the Slovak population. Moreover, we must take into account the qualitative level of the mentioned issue of the brain drain. The data from the Table 1 show it clearly.

The low representation of educated people among the Slovak emigrants is alarming. In 2014, the share of educated people in the total number of emigrants from Slovakia represented 28.1%, and it was significantly higher than the share of employed university graduates in Slovakia (19.84%).

Table 1 Comparison of education structure of emigrants with the working population in Slovakia

Education	Leaving the Slovak Republic	Working in the Slovak Republic
Basic (%)	3.45	5.72
Vocational without GCE (%)	16.05	30.82
Vocational and secondary with GCE (%)	52.4	43.61
University (%)	28.10	19.84

Source Own calculations based on the data from the Statistical Office of the Slovak Republic (2014, p. 32) and the Labor Force Survey

There are more reasons for which our experts decide to work in another country. A significant position among them is the low salary for many important professions such as doctors, teachers, and researchers. Another significant reason is the serious gap in Slovakia regarding support of SME and start-ups. There is an absence of appropriate legislation that would support this type of business environment. In the case of a suitable business environment in Slovakia, a young person would easily find a job that would have brought him, in addition to financial remuneration, a feeling of inner satisfaction. Alternatively, he or she could even start his or her own business. Young people have many new ideas. If they cannot realize them at home, they try often their luck abroad where they find a greater support.

Insufficient quality of some universities in Slovakia is also one of many factors that cause difficulties in finding a job for Slovak university graduates. Slovakia is characterized by a relatively high number of universities (relative to the total number of inhabitants). This results in a degradation of the university degree such that even outstanding graduates have difficulties in finding an adequate job. In this situation, many of them decide to emigrate hoping that they will find a job.

Foreign students are a kind of precursor of highly qualified migrant workers. Therefore, a part of the research of brain drain should include also a trend in the evolution of the number of Slovak students studying abroad.

At the turn of the year from 2014 to 2015, the Sociological Institute of the Slovak Academy of Sciences, in cooperation with the Faculty of Social and Economic Sciences at the Comenius University, performed a research named Brain Drain in 2014, which resulted in the following conclusions (Bahna 2015):

- Students studying abroad are represented significantly more by graduates of secondary bilingual schools.
- Slovaks studying abroad come mainly from families with above-average level of human capital. Almost a half of them comes from families in which both parents have a university education. Compared with students studying in Slovakia, the proportion is three times higher.
- The main reasons for the decision to study abroad are the reputation of foreign schools and the belief that a diploma from a prestigious university is a good way to find a better job.

An important outcome of the research are also the reasons which help to decide to the university graduate abroad whether or not he or she returns to Slovakia:

- If both parents have a university degree, this increases the probability that the child will remain abroad.
- Most parents with an only child desire that their child return home.
    - In contrast, parents of the children who attended secondary bilingual schools do not insist on return.

5 Conclusions

Evolution in the Slovak labor market is a key issue in both the short- and long-term development of the Slovak economy. Indicators of employment and unemployment occupy leading positions in the evaluation of the social situation of the population and in the perception of living standards of the population. From a macroeconomic perspective, the main trends in the labor market are optimistic. The forecast of development confirm that the positive trend will continue in the following years.

The Commission recommends in all its documents to reduce the tax burden, with no impact on the budget, which should be achieved by an increase of the environmental, consumption, and property taxes. In this measure, a positive impact is expected in the long term, especially for the most vulnerable groups in the labor market as well as for low-income workers. Investment in human capital and reform of education and training system focused on that results are part of the necessary effort to restore jobs and a sustainable growth.

The problem of migration of qualified labor and the related brain drain is one of the biggest challenges of the twenty first century. It is also concerning to Slovakia. In this paper, we performed a more detailed analysis of the factors affecting the brain drain from Slovakia, and we also outlined specific solutions that are applicable in practice.

References

Bahna M (2015) Slovenski absolventi vysokoskolskeho studia v zahranici. Unik mozgov, alebo otvarajuce sa mobilitne kanaly na Slovensku? Pracovne texty 1. Sociologicky ustav SAV, Bratislava

Bleha B, Vano B (2007) Niektore teoreticke a metodologicke aspekty populacnej politiky a nacrt jej koncepcie pre Slovensku republiku. https://www.sav.sk/journals/uploads/02031258Vano%20-%20Bleha.pdf. Accessed 3 Mar 2007

Divinsky B (2014) Migracia zo Slovenskej republiky od roku 2004: vybrane crty, existujuce vyzvy, navrhy rieseni. https://www.researchgate.net/publication/266527580_Migracia_zo_Slovenskej_republiky_od_roku_2004_vybrane_crty_existujuce_vyzvy_navrhy_rieseni. Accessed Aug 12 2015

Europska komisia (2016) Sprava o krajine za rok 2016 Slovensko. SWD. 93 final

Kostelecka Y, Bernard J (2007) Zahranicni migrace vedcu a vyzkumniku a nastroje k jejimu ovlivneni. Sociologicky ustav AV CR, Praha

Lubyova M, Stefanik M et al (2015) Trh prace na Slovensku 2016+. Ekonomicky ustav SAV, Bratislava

Rievajova E et al (2015) Trh prace—premeny a vyzvy. EKONOM, Bratislava

Tiruneh W, Stefanik MM et al (2014) Trh prace na Slovensku: Analyza a prognozy. Ekonomicky ustav SAV, Bratislava

USZZ (2008) Koncepcia statnej politiky starostlivosti o Slovakov zijucich v zahranici do roku 2014. Urad pre Slovakov zijucich v zahranici. Uznesenie vlady SR No. 625/2008, Bratislava

Portion of Foreign Ownership and Efficiency of Banks in Indonesia

Sparta

Abstract This study aimed to accomplish the following: (1) determine the foreign ownership in a private national bank and a non-foreign exchange bank; (2) determine the impact of foreign ownership on the efficiency of the national private banking and non-foreign exchange; and (3) determine if there are differences in the impact of the percentage of foreign ownership of a bank on the efficiency of national private groups and non-foreign exchange. The samples are comprised of banks in the group of Foreign-Exchange National Private Bank (BUSND) and the National Private Bank Non-Foreign Exchange (BUSNND). The number of banks that became the subject of research include as many as 54 banks from the period 2001–2013 with the total number of observations being 702; however, the number of observations included in the data processing is 648. This is due to the use of variable BOPO in the previous year, so the data BOPO was 1 year before starting 2002. Research variables used are BOPO, share of foreign ownership, bank size, and group dummy variables. The equation used is OLS research using panel data. The results of this study prove the following: (1) Foreign ownership has a positive influence on inefficiencies for a particular group of BUSND and BUSNND; (2) the greater the bank's assets, the more efficient the bank tends to be; and (3) there is no difference in the impact of foreign ownership on bank-efficiency levels among the BUSND and BUSNN groups. The results of this study have implications for the policy to restrict foreign ownership in national banks. Revisions of the Banking Act, one of which is to limit foreign ownership in national banks, are being processed in the Commission XI. The results of this study can be considered in the revision of the Banking Law. Foreign ownership is a particular point because increased foreign ownership tends to decrease banking system efficiency.

Keywords Foreign ownership · The bank's assets · BUSND · BUSNND · Banking law

Sparta (✉)
Accounting Department, Indonesia Banking School, Jalan Kemang Raya No.35, Kemang, South Jakarta 12730, Indonesia
e-mail: Sparta@ibs.ac.id
URL: http://www.ibs.ac.id

E. Lau et al. (eds.), *Selected Papers from the Asia-Pacific Conference on Economics & Finance (APEF 2016)*, DOI 10.1007/978-981-10-3566-1_9

1 Introduction

Since the banking regulations on foreign ownership issued by Bank Indonesia through Act 29 of 1999, foreign investors have been allowed to own national banks ($\geq$99% ownership), has become a trigger mastered by the foreign banking industry. This condition would not be healthy and would affect the development of the national banking system.

The regulation of foreign ownership in Indonesian banks is considered less strict compared with that in other countries. China have 30% foreign ownership in their banking sector (http://www.ibpa.co.id/News/) according to the research of Hawes and Chiu (2007; in Rusdi; November 2014 [http://kinerjabank.com/kepemilikan-asing-di-perbankan-indonesia/]). Foreign ownership in Chinese banks from 2005 until 2006 reached 19.9%. This foreign ownership portion describes is the ownership of HSBC in Bank of Communication. Likewise, Saudi Arabia has a 40% maximum limit for foreign ownership in their banking sector. In Malaysia, for example, Bank Negara Malaysia (BNM) limits collective ownership to $\leq$30%. Compositions include a single foreign company with a maximum of 20% foreign ownership, whereas foreign individuals can have $\leq$10% ownership. Thailand and the Philippines have also implemented similar policies. In Thailand, foreigners can own shares of a bank $\leq$100%. However, in 10 years the investor must divest its stake to the remaining 49%. In the Philippines, foreigners are also allowed to hold shares up to 100%, but after 7 years they should be lowered to 40% (http://fokus.kontan.co.id/news/menanti-pagar-pembatas-asing-di-industri-perbankan).

What is the proportion foreign ownership in national banks in Indonesia since the crisis up until now? Some current data on foreign bank ownership include the following: (a) Bank CIMB Niaga is 97% owned by CIMB Malaysia; (b) Bank Danamond is 67% owned by Temasek of Singapore; (c) Bank BII is 80% owned by Malaysia's Maybank; (d) Bank OCBC NISP is 81.1% owned by OCBC Singapore; and (e) Bank UOB Buana is 98.9% owned by UOB Singapore (DER 2014).

The entry of foreign investors into the Indonesia banking industry can not be separated from the impact of the global crisis during 1997–1998. During the crisis, the majority of capital injection into banking sector was from foreign investors, whereas local investors were afraid to invest their capital even though Bank Indonesia has offered them to be shareholders.

What does the increase in the percentage of foreign ownership actually contribute to the national banking system, especially in terms of improving the efficiency and financial performance of bank and vice versa?

Previous research linking the portion of foreign ownership to the financial performance of banks, performed by Bonin et al. (2003), found evidence that a significant relationship exists between foreign ownership and bank performance in the transition countries of the Soviet Union. Research addressing the effect of foreign ownership on bank performance was performed by Rahman and Reza (2015) in Malaysia during 2000–2011 and concluded that there was no effect. Another study was performed by Swai and Mbogela (2014) in Tanzania during 2000–2009, and the results showed that foreign ownership has not significantly influenced k performance.

Foreign ownership in national banks has an influence on the efficiency of the national banking system. Research performed by Berger et al. (2008) shows that the Big Four banks in China showed lower levels of efficiency compared with foreign banks. A low level of foreign ownership in major China banks can improve the efficiency of the banks as well as their financial performance. These results are similar to those of study performed by Laurenceson and Qin (2008), which proved that foreign ownership of banks in China has an influence on their efficiency, particularly significant in terms of cost. Mardanugraha (2005) concluded that during 1993–2003, joint-venture banks (foreign and national ownership) were more efficient than locally owned banks in Indonesia. The different results in Beck's research, compared with those from Beck and Hesse (2006) on banking in Uganda in 1999–2005, show that an increase in foreign ownership of banks does not increase banking efficiency in the country. DeYoung and Nolle (1996) showed that foreign-bank branches in the USA from 1985 to 1990 had a less-efficient profit compared with a local bank owned by a citizen of USA. This is because foreign owned banks use more expensive input than locally owned banks. This evidence suggests that foreign-owned banks are less likely to draw and maintain local customers than locally owned banks due to the expensive cost of funds. The results of research by DeYoung and Nolle (1996), together with the results of research performed by Sans et al. (2011) in Malaysia, shows that foreign banks are less efficient than local banks.

Based on the previous results, it is necessary to perform research to prove the impact of the percentage of foreign ownership on the efficiency of national private banks of the foreign and non-foreign exchanges. The study was performed in this particular bank group because foreign ownership has its greatest variation in this bank group. State-owned, joint-venture, foreign, and regional development banks lacked variation as to high share of foreign ownership. For example, regional-development banks, are in majority owned by local government, whereas foreign ownership in the banks "*persero*" have relatively little foreign ownership.

This study examined annual data period from 2001 to 2013. This was due to the availability of existing data and the time constraint.

Based on the notes, research problems included the following:

1. What is the image of foreign ownership in national private banks of the foreign exchange and the non-foreign exchange?
2. What is the impact of the change in foreign-ownership percentage on the efficiency of national private banks of the foreign exchange and non-foreign exchange when bank size is he controlled variable?
3. Is there any difference in the percentage of foreign influence on national private banks of the foreign exchange and non-foreign exchange regarding bank efficiency?

2 Literature Review

2.1 *Efficiency Bank*

Banking efficiency is measured by calculating the difference between the minimum cost of banking with cost that should be issued by the bank to produce the same output (Mardanugraha 2005). The minimum fee is obtained from the estimated minimum cost of banking functions. Bank efficiency can be divided into two types: technical efficiency and allocative efficiency (Farel 1957). Pindyck and Rubinfeld (1995) divides the efficiency in terms of economic efficiency into two: technical efficiency and price efficiency. Allocative efficiency is the efficiency of the economy related to the efficiency of the price-related cost function. Economic efficiency is achieved in the event of technical efficiency and the efficiency of the price (or allocative efficiency).

There are several methods of measuring the efficiency of banking, namely,

- The traditional approach uses index or ratios such as return on assets (ROA), capital adequacy ratio (CAR), profitability ratio, and the ratio of operating expenses to operating income (BOPO).
- The frontier approach is based on the optimal behavior of the company in order to maximize output or minimize costs as a way to achieve the goal of economic unit (Hartono 2009). The frontier approach consists of: (a) deterministic approach (non-parametric approach), which uses TEKHNICAL Mathematic Programming or with popular data-envelopment analysis (DEA).
- The stochastic approach is classified as a parametric approach using an econometric frontier.

In this study, the ratio used for bank efficiency measurement is the BOPO ratio. There are several reasons why the BOPO ratio is used: First, the ratio is widely used by the banking industry and the institutions banking authority (FSA) in assessing the efficiency of a bank. Second, the ratio is provided in the annual financial statements of banks. Third, determination of the ratio is much simpler. Weaknesses in using the BOPO ratio is that this ratio illustrates the level of efficiency of banks individually without considering the average costs and revenues of the other banks.

2.2 *Influence of Foreign Ownership Structure on Bank Efficiency*

In recent years, the relationship between ownership and performance in the industrial non-banking industry has been developed in the literature (Altunbas et al. 2001). The performance of the banking industry is seen from the level of efficiency achieved by the bank. There are two messages from the literature review: The nature bank ownership is very important, and the study of the theory helps to look at the issues in the context of the framework of principal-agent theory and public-choice theory.

In the agency theory, which was first disclosed by Jensen and Meckling (1976), the owner has turned over the management of economic resources to the manager. Company performance, however, did not cause problem of any agency; it depends not on the owner or the manager of the corporate-ownership structure (Jensen and Meckling 1976). Empirical results show inconsistencies with agency theory, in which a company's performance can be affected by the ownership structure of the company. Efficiency is included in the company's performance. Here we present some empirical results regarding the relationship between ownership structure and bank efficiency.

The ownership structure of different banks will provide a different level of efficiency for each bank (Awdeh and El Moussawi 2009; Shaher et al. 2011). The research results on banks in the State of Lebanon from 1996 to 2005 showed that the majority of foreign-owned banks have greater improvement in efficiency levels compared with the majority of locally owned banks In other words, locally owned banks have a weaker performance than foreign-owned banks

Research on foreign ownership and bank efficiency was also performed by Rajput and Gupta (2011) in India. Of 32 foreign banks surveyed in India during 2005–2010, there was an increase in the efficiency of foreign-owned banks. The ease and opportunities given by central bank authorities to foreign banks led to a growing expansion of foreign banks. Four years after the space given in April 2009 by India's central bank, there was rapid growth in the performance of foreign banks. These results are consistent with research performed by Berger et al. (2008) on the structure of foreign ownership of major banks in China. The results showed that the efficiency of foreign-owned banks are better than those of state owned banks. The same thing also happened in Indonesia in 1993–2003, which was investigated by Mardanugraha (2005) and by Abidin (2007) for the period 2002–2005. The same study performed by Bonin et al. (2003) in former countries Yugoslavia and the Soviet Union found that foreign-owned banks more efficient than state- and private-owned banks.

The results of different ongoing studies of Uganda's foreign-owned banks show that foreign ownership of banks in the country does not improve banking efficiency (Beck and Hesse 2006). Furthermore, Beck and Hesse found that the increase in foreign ownership of banks in Uganda did not increase the spread or margin of banks in the country such that the performance of foreign-owned banks did not increase. The results of the research in Uganda are similar to the results of research on foreign banks in the USA for different reasons, which shows the level of efficiency of foreign-owned banks in the USA to be lower than those of banks owned by local residents (DeYoung and Nolle 1996). Foreign banks in the United States were not able to obtain cheaper funds for their input. The more expensive inputs led to decreasing financial performance, or no better than locally owned banks, of foreign-owned banks.

Studies on the effect of government ownership on bank efficiency, performed by Altunbas et al. (2001) on 1195 private commercial banks (2858 public saving banks and 3486 mutual co-operative banks) contained observations in Germany. The result showed that banks owned by the private sector are more efficient than government-owned banks. Further research is also inconsistent with the Agency Theory, in which the performance of the company is not determined by the ownership structure but rather depends on the company manager (Hadad et al. 2003). Results of research by Hadad et al. (2003) show no link between structure of ownership in Indonesian banks with the bank's performance. In this condition, the Agency Theory can be applied.

Based on the results of the study of theory and previous research results, the hypothesis are as follows:

Ha1: Foreign Ownership Affects Bank Efficiency

2.3 The Influence of Bank Size on Bank Efficiency

McAllister and McManus (1993; in Iannotta et al. [2006]) showed that the major banks have an opportunity to diversify risk; thus, major banks have lower cost of funds compared with small banks. Large banks tend to earn higher net interest income compared with smaller banks. This fact is associated with high economies of scale in large banks compared with small banks because cheaper funds are more easily obtained in the money market. In addition, the level of market and the public confidence to entrust their funds to large banks is higher than for small banks. Despite that cost of funds is lower for large banks than small banks, more people tend to save their money in large banks. Thus, the economies of scale or size in banking are positively correlated with efficiency.

In terms of credit management, large banks tend to have lower levels of efficiency than smaller banks. There is no large difference in costs between large credit-management firms and small loan-management firms (Ramli 2005). Large banks have greater credit amount than small banks. Thus, the efficiency level of large banks tends to be greater compared with smaller banks.

According to economic theory, the relationship between input and output changes is described in terms of increasing returns to scale, decreasing returns to scale, and constant returns to scale (Pindyck and Rubinfield 1995). Large banks with increasing returns to scale have higher levels of efficiency than smaller banks. In contrast, large banks with decreasing returns to scale have lower levels level of efficiency than smaller banks. In conditions of constant return to scale, large banks and small banks have the same the level of inefficiency.

With the theory study as well as the previous study, the research hypothesis proposed are as follows:

Ha2: Bank Size Affects Bank Efficiency

2.4 *Differences Regarding the Influence of Bank Eficiency*

The size of the group of national private non-foreign exchange banks is less than the group of national private foreign-exchange banks (Mardanugraha 2005). In advance, first, the capital and asset requirement are greater in foreign-exchange national private banks than in non-foreign exchange national private banks (Hadad et al. 2003). Second, the operational activities of foreign-exchange national private banks are broader than those of non-foreign exchange national private banks. Thus, the research hypothesis related to differences in the efficiency of two private bank groups is as follows:

Ha3: Differences Exist in the Effect of Foreign Ownership on Efficiency of the BUSND Group Versus the BUSNND Group

3 Methodology

This research use samples of foreign-exchange and non-foreign exchange national private banks derived from the commercial bank population. The sample used in this research are all existing banks in the group of non-foreign exchange and foreign-exchange national private sector during 2001–2013. The number of commercial banks in Indonesia that participated in this the study (13 years) includes 914 observations (Table 1).

The number of banks presented in the table were banks with a complete set of financial statements during the study period. Bank mergers, conventional banks that

Table 1 Number of sample research 2001–2013

Years	Commercial bank		Sample (*n*)
	BUSNND	BUSND	
2001	38	42	80
2002	36	40	76
2003	36	40	76
2004	35	38	73
2005	34	37	71
2006	35	36	71
2007	35	36	71
2008	35	33	68
2009	34	31	65
2010	36	31	67
2011	36	30	66
2012	35	30	65
2013	35	30	65

Source Data of Indonesia Banking Statistics (Bank Indonesia)

were converted into Islamic banks, and banks that had their license revoked were not included in this study. The data used are balance panel data. Twenty-five foreign-exchange national private banks group had complete financial statements banks. Twenty-nine non-foreign exchange national private banks had complete financial statements. The 2 groups total 54 banks. Seven hundred two observations were studied (54 banks × 13 years).

The data used in this study were derived from the annual financial statements of banks in the Indonesia Bank Directory from January 2001 to December 2013. The data in the financial statements are required to determine the share of foreign ownership, bank efficiency, and bank size. The data were taken from the Indonesian banking directory the period 2001–2013 and were grouped into (1) Foreign exchange national private banks (BUSND) and (2) non-foreign exchange national private banks (BUSNND). Definitions of variables used in this study are briefly presented in Table 2. Equation study are as follows:

In the panel data, it is important to distinguish whether the panel-data regression model is fitted using a common-effect model (CEM), fixed-effect model (FEM), or random-effect model (REM). A Chow test and Housman test on the panel-data regression equation were required (Gujarati 2003). Several classic tests include (1) residual normality test by Kolmogorov–Smirnof, (2) multicollinearity test, (3) autocorrelation test and (4) heteroscedasticity test.

Hypothesis testing was performed using Student *t* test (partial test). Analysis of the explanatory power of the independent variables explains the variation of the dependent variable and was performed by looking at the amount of adjusted R^2 models. The significance level of the Student *t* test is in the alpha at 1, 5, or 10%.

Table 2 Definition and variable operational research

No	Variable	Definition	Indicator	Scale
1	Bank efficiency	Ratio of operating expenses to operating income (BOPO)	=Operating expense/operating income	Ratio
2	Foreign ownership	Percentage of foreign ownership of total outstanding shares of the banks (POWNFR)	=(Number of foreign shares)/total outstanding shares of the bank ×100%	Ratio
3	Bank size	Total Bank assets at the reporting date (LNASSET)	=Natural logarithm of total asset	Ratio
4	Dummy-bank group	Two groups of foreign-exchange private banks and non-foreign exchange private banks (DBank)	The dummy number is 1 when entering the national private banks, and the foreign-exchange dummy number is 0 when in the group of non-foreign national private banks	

Source Adapted own

4 Results and Discussion

4.1 Overview of Research Sample

The research sample consisted of 54 banks from 2001 to 2013 (i.e., 13-year period) so that the total number of observations is 702. The number of observations included in the data processing was 648 for their variable POWNFR at 1 year before being used so that the data POWNFR at 1 year before begins in 2002. The number of banks surveyed were from two groups of banks: national private foreign-exchange banks (n = 25) and national private non-foreign exchange banks (n = 29). This was done because both groups have a share of foreign ownership that is quite high compared with state-owned banks and regional-development banks. Foreign banks and joint-venture banks were not included in the sample because of foreign ownership: Especially foreign banks are stagnant and the average foreign ownership is close to 100%.

From Table 3, the average efficiency of the banks using BOPO is 87.67%. On average during the last 12 years, private foreign-exchange and non-foreign exchange banks have not been efficient. This is because the average BOPO is still above the average BOPO of banks in ASEAN. From the research data, the most efficient banks by BOPO is a group of private bank-foreign exchange banks, namely, PT Alfindo Sejahtera Bank with BOPO = 0.4082, whereas the most inefficient is a private non-foreign exchange bank, namely, PT Bank Sri Partha with BOPO = 1.9070.

The average percentage of foreign ownership in national private banks, both foreign-exchange and non-foreign exchange, was 18.7%. The portion of foreign

Table 3 Statistic descriptive research (2011–2013)

	BOPO	POWNFR	TASSET	LNASSET	DSTATUS	RESID
Mean	0.876729	0.186960	16,927,388	14.63834	0.495370	1.22E−18
Median	0.873600	0.000000	1693092.	14.34207	0.000000	−0.003519
Maximum	1.907000	0.990000	4.88E+08	20.00685	1.000000	0.637363
Minimum	0.408200	0.000000	19,443.00	9.875242	0.000000	−0.569227
SD	0.147045	0.323639	46,439,459	2.008170	0.500365	0.101607
Skewness	1.817139	1.418435	5.595881	0.441181	0.018519	1.141574
Kurtosis	12.43637	3.406273	43.28595	2.491382	1.000343	12.45823
Sum	568.1207	121.1500	1.10E+10	9485.647	321.0000	6.45E−16
Sum SD	13.98953	67.76803	1.40E+18	2609.187	161.9861	6.679625
Observations (n)	648	648	648	648	648	648
Cross-sections	54	54	54	54	54	54

Resource Result of statitstic process

ownership in one national private bank, namely PT Bank Buana Indonesia, is 99%. The lowest portion of foreign ownership is 0% at several banks in the two groups (BUSND and BUSNND).

Banks with the largest assets are those of a national private foreign-exchange commercial banks, namely, Bank Central Asia with total assets of Rp. 488.5 trillion in 2013, whereas banks with the fewest assets is a national private non-foreign exchange commercial bank, namely, PT Bank Alfindo Sejahtera with total assets of Rp. 19.4 billion.

Bank status is a dummy variable for the bank group, and equals 1 for BUSND or 0 for the BUSNND bank group. The first group of banks (BUSND) consists of 25 banks, and the second group (BUSNND) consists of 29 banks. Thus, the obtained the average value of this dummy variable is 0.4954. The result is closer to 0 than to 1 because the number of banks that have 0 dummy value are greater than the banks with a dummy value of 1.

4.2 Overview of the Portion of Foreign Ownership in Private Foreign-Exchange and Non-foreign Exchange Banks in 2001–2013

The average share of foreign ownership per year in the group of BUSND and BUSNDD banks increased during 2001–2013 (see Fig. 1). It was not separate from the improvement of the Indonesian economy during that period, and the regulation of foreign ownership in commercial banks in Indonesia is not as strict compared with other countries in ASEAN. Foreign ownership in BUSND and BUSNND banks in 2013 reached 28.57%. This portion is well above the average share of foreign ownership in the State of Malaysia, which has a 30% maximum limit of foreign ownership as does China. China's proportion of foreign ownership in 2006 reached 19.9%

4.3 Overview of Bank Efficiency in Private Foreign-Exchange and Non-foreign Exchange Banks in 2001–2013

How are the conditions of banking efficiency of BUSND and BUSNND-group banks? By using BOPO as of banking efficiency measurement, the BOPO ratio of banks in the two groups per year on average showed a tendency to decrease (Fig. 2). In other words, the level of banking efficiency has a positive trend. Both aggregated and separated data of the two groups show equal results. BUSNND group banks on average appear to have better levels of efficiency compared with

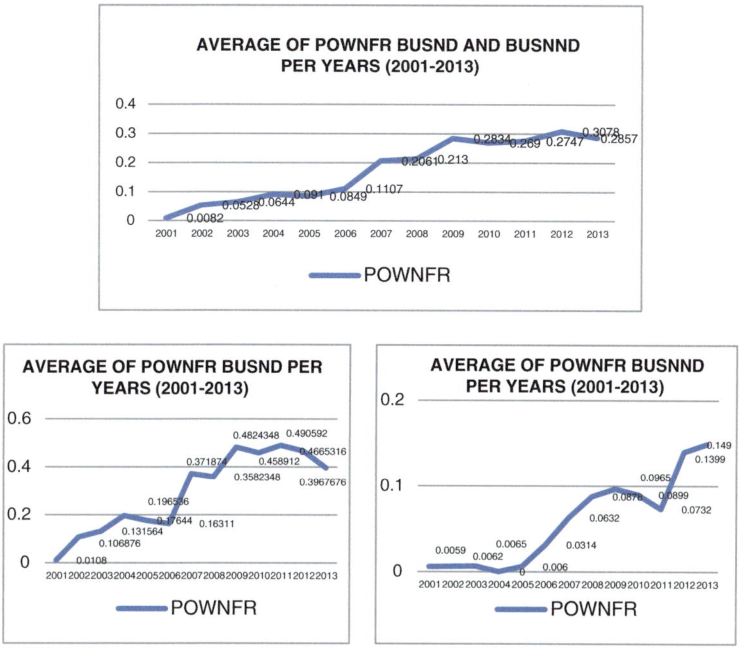

Fig. 1 Overview of the Portion of Foreign Ownership in BUSND and BUSNND Banks in Indonesia in 2001–2013

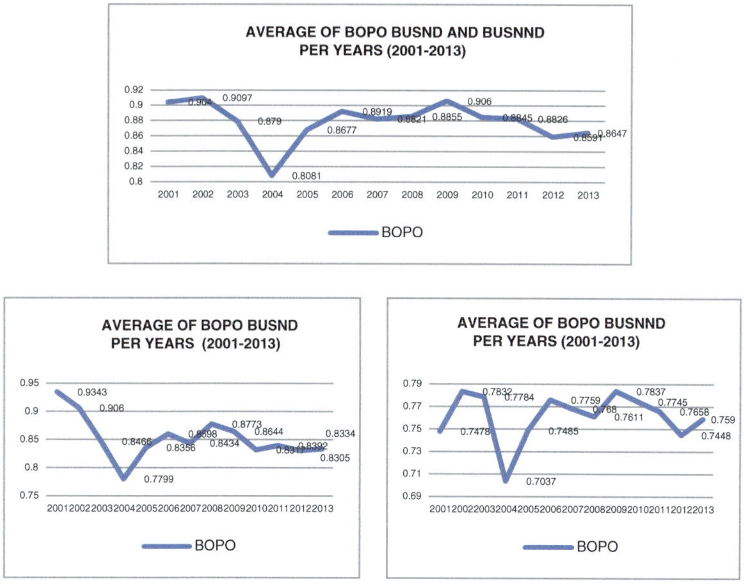

Fig. 2 Picture of efficiency in banking. BUSND and BUSNND Groups in Indonesia (2001–2013)

BUSND banks. However, regarding individual bank level, the increasing trend of efficiency level has not yet been proven.

4.4 Results of Regression Equation

Regression results using the Fixed-Effect Model with OLS equations using panel data after the Chow test and Housman test are listed in Table 4. OLS regression results using fixed-effect panel data (see the output results attached) show that the portion of the effect of foreign ownership, or a significant positive BOPO, significantly reduces the level of bank efficiency. The higher the share of foreign ownership, the more inefficient the BUSNND and BUSND group banks become. The size of the banks in both groups negatively affects the BOPO: The bigger the bank, the more efficient the bank. The effect of foreign ownership on bank efficiency is not significantly different between the two groups. This is evident from the significance of the group dummy variable, which is not significant at alpha 5%. The ability of independent variables to explain the variation of changes in BOPO or the adjusted R^2 is 59.66% (Table 4).

Table 4 Regression equation result with fixed-effect balance data panel-dependent variable BOPO method: pooled least squares white cross-section depicts SEs and covariance (no d*f* correction)

Variable	Coefficient SE	Student *t*-statistic *p*	Description
C	0.774852 0.136278	5.685818*** 0.0000	
BOPO(−1)	0.400277 0.054089	7.400352*** 0.0000	+
POWNFR	0.060855 0.024503	2.483538*** 0.0133	+
LNASSET	−0.019012 0.008777	−2.166225*** 0.0307	−
DSTATUS	0.033437 0.025345	1.319275 0.1876	
R^2	0.632097		
Adjusted R^2	0.596554		
F-statistic	17.78395		
probability	0.000000***		
Durbin–Watson statistic	1.957036		
Cross-sections included:	54		
Total pool of (balanced) observations:	648		

Source Processed by the statistical program
*Significant at alpha 10%;**Significant at alpha 5%; ***Significant at alpha 1%

Table 5 Correlation between the variable research

	BOPO	POWNFR	TASSET	LNASSET	DSATUS
BOPO	1	–	–	–	–
POWNFR	0.05487	1	–	–	–
TASSET	−0.22643	0.3201	1	–	–
LNASSET	−0.22456	0.4411	0.63691	1	–
DSATUS	−0.14760	0.33228	0.32127	0.63578	1

Source Processed by the statistical program

Assuming a central limit theorem where the research number of 648 exceeds the 30 observational data, the residual normality test is not required in this study (Wooldrige 2005). It is assumed that the data are 648, so the data are normally distributed.

Multicollinearity symptoms can be seen by using the correlation between the independent variables. Table 5 lists the correlation between variables, which is still far below 0.8. Therefore, there are no signs of multicollinearity in previous regression results.

Test symptoms underwent autocorrelation using Durbin–Watson (DW) test. Based on Table 4, the statistic number of DW is 1.957036; therefore, there are no signs of autocorrelation in the previous regression results.

Heteroscedasticity test was not performed in this research because the white cross-section SEs and covariance panel data equation regression were used. By using the white cross-section, heteroscedasticity on SE and covariance occurring in the previous regression equation can be avoided (Woodrige 2005).

Based on the regression results listed in Table 4, the Ha1 hypothesis is unacceptable at a positive level of significance at alpha = 0.0133. The coefficient parameter of POWNFR was 0.061. This means that a change of one unit of foreign ownership will increase the BOPO level by 0.061 or decrease the level of BUNND and BUND efficiency. The Ha2 hypothesis can be accepted at a negative significance level of alpha = 0.0307, and the parameter of the variable LNSIZE was −2.166. This means that increasing LNSIZE by one unit will decrease the BOPO level of 2166 or will increase the level of BUSND bank efficiency to 2166. The unacceptable Ha3 hypothesis means that the influence of foreign ownership on bank efficiency is no difference compared between the two groups of banks.

4.5 *Analysis of the Effect of Proportion of Foreign Ownership on Bank Efficiency*

The results of this study prove empirically that the proportion of foreign ownership has a significant positive influence on the inefficiency of BUSND and BUSNND banks. The results of the study support the results of research performed by Beck and Hesse (2006) and DeYoung and Nolle (1996), i.e., that foreign ownership is not able to improve the efficiency of banks. Foreign banks in the USA are less efficient than local banks (DeYoung and Nolle 1996) because foreign banks have more expensive input value compared with local banks. Foreign banks are not able to attract and maintain customers in the country, so the cost of funding is more expensive. This condition also occurs in Indonesia. Indonesia's banks with a higher level of foreign ownership were not able to increase their efficiency because the government and the national bank customers prefer to make transactions with locally owned banks. The same thing is true regarding the research Sans et al. (2011) in Malaysia, who suggest that banks with increased foreign ownership are less efficient compared with locally owned banks.

The results of this study differ from the those of Berger et al. (2008), Laurenceson and Qin (2008). Awdeh and El Moussawi (2009); in Shaher et al. (2011), Rajput and Gupta (2011), Mardanugraha (2005), and Abidin (2007). Study results from Berger et al. (2008) proved that an increase in the proportion of minority interest of foreign ownership in China increases the level of efficiency of the banks. Foreign banks in China have a higher level of efficiency than state-owned banks included in the Big Four banks. Mardanugraha (2005) proved during 1993–2003 that joint-venture banks (foreign and national ownership) are more efficient than national banks. Differences in the research results of Mardanugraha with those of research performed empirically are due to differences in the time period and the study sample. The research period of Mardanugraha was 1993–2003, whereas this study covered 2001–2013. The study period of 1993 and 2003 include the periods before and after the financial crisis of 1998, at which time nearly all national bank experienced a decrease in performance due to problem loans.

Associated with Agency Theory, the results of this study show that the performance and efficiency of banks are still affected by foreign ownership. Foreign owners still intervene in bank operations. Banks managers, as agents, are not free to mange their banks. Agency Theory does not apply to national private foreign-exchange banks and national private non-foreign exchange banks.

4.6 Analysis of the Effect of Bank Size on Bank Efficiency

This study proves that bank size can have a negative impact on bank ROA ratio or a positive impact on bank efficiency. Large banks tend to be more efficient than smaller banks because large banks have the opportunity to diversify their products, posses an extensive network, and have a high-enough level of public confidence to be able to obtain cheaper funds (third-party funds as saving and deposit) compared with small banks. This argument is according to McAllister and McManus (1993; in Iannotta et al. [2006]). In terms of credit management, large banks have a large credit volume with a fewer number of debtors, so the cost of credit management is not much different from the management of small credit (Ramli 2005). This also shows that BUNSD and BUSNND-group banks have the condition of increasing to scale. Increasing the volume of banking operations could still improve acceleration results. Regarding input and output, conditions of increasing to scale showed that the change rate of the input is twice to increase output more than double that efficiency has increased higher (Pindyck and Rubinfield 1995).

4.7 Differential Analysis of the Effect of the Proportion of Foreign Ownership on Bank Efficiency in National Private Foreign-Exchange and Non-foreign Exchange Banks

This study proves that there is no difference in linking efficiency to foreign ownership in the two groups of banks that were examined during 2001–2013. That is, the negative impact of foreign ownership on the efficiency of the banks does not distinguish itself in BUSND versus BUSNND-group banks. Thus, the impact of foreign ownership on bank efficiency for both groups is either the same or not significantly different.

The increase in foreign ownership in the banks studied during the period 2001–2013 (13-year period) increased from 0.82% in 2001 to 28.57% in 2013. This increase would also decrease the efficiency of the two groups of banks in general.

4.8 Managerial-Implications Research

The negative impact of foreign ownership on the efficiency of BUSNND and BUSND-group banks has negative implications for management. The authorities should take into consideration a policy to restrict foreign ownership in banking in Indonesia. Foreign ownership has consistently increased from 2001 to 2013 and provides a potential decline in the performance of Indonesian banks. Putting restrictions on foreign ownership has been debated in the revision of the Banking Law Commission XI DPRI RI. These empirical results prove that foreign-ownership restrictions should be limited to neighboring countries such as Malaysia, Thailand, Philippines, China, India, and other countries. Restrictions on 40% foreign ownership is desirable in some quarters in the revision of the Banking Act are still a strong proposal (www.sinarharapan.com/news/read/150612075/-ownership of foreign-bank-in-so-debate).

The research proves that large banks tend to be more efficient than small banks. These results have implications for banking authorities to institute a policy of merging smaller banks into big banks so as to ready to compete with ASEAN countries in dealing with the Asean Economic Community (AEC) in 2020. If mergers are not performed, then when the AEC is applied to the banking sector in

2020. Banks in Indonesia will find it difficult to compete because the other ASEAN countries have fewer banks yet greater assets than Indonesia's banks.

5 Conclusions, Limitations, and Suggestions

In summary, the current research proves the following:

- The greater the portion of foreign ownership, the more inefficient the bank.
- Increasing in the bank's assets will increase more than ever before.
- There is no difference in the effect of proportion of foreign ownership on efficiency of BUSND versus BUSNND-group banks.

The implication of the results of this study is the need for policies restricting foreign ownership in national banks. Revisions to the Banking Act are being processed in the Commission XI, one of which is to limit the proportion of foreign ownership in national banks. The results of this study can be considered in the revision of the Banking Law, particularly regarding foreign ownership, because of increased foreign ownership tends to reduce the efficiency of banks in Indonesia.

The measure of efficiency used is BOPO, which incidentally is derived from bank accounting data. Different accounting practices used in each bank caused BOPO figures to not be comparable from one bank to another. There is a need to measure efficiency using a stochastic approach. This measurement approach is capable to produce equal-size efficiency among banks.

This study examined only two independent variables; in the next study, we expect have more independent variables. Other independent variables that can be considered are risk of banking, capital, and macroeconomic indicators.

References

Abidin Z (2007) Performance efficiency of commercial bank. In: Proceedings PESAT (psychology, economics, literature, architects and civil), vol 2, ISSN 1858-2559, August, it A113–119
Altunbas Y, Evans L, Molyneux P (2001) Bank ownership and efficiency. J Money, Credit Bank 33(4):927–954
Awdeh A, El Moussawi C (2009) Bank efficiency and foreign ownership in the lebanese banking sector. Rev Meddle East Econ Fin 5(2)
Bank Indonesia, Bank Indonesia Regulation No. 13/I/PBI/2011 dated January 5, 2011 on the level of health, (2011) through thehttp://www.bi.go.id/
Beck T, Hesse H (2006) Bank efficiency, ownership and market structure-why are so high interest spreads in Uganda. In: World Bank policy research working paper 4027, via http://econ.worldbank.org
Berger AN, Iftekhar H, Mingming Z (2008) Bank ownership and efficiency in China: what will happen in the world's largest nation? J Bank Fin 1–18. doi:10.1016/j.jbankfin.2007.05.016
Bonin JP, Hasan I, Wachtel P (2003) Bank performance, efficiency, and ownership in transition countries. In: Paper presented in the ninth Dubrovnik economic conference the 9 DEC.

Banking and the financial Sector in transition and emerging market economic, organized by The Croatian National Bank, in Dubrovnik, 26–28 June 2003

DeYoung R, Nolle DE (1996) Foreign-owned bank in the USA: earning market share or buying it? J Money, Credit Bank 28:622–636

Farel, MJ (1957) The measurement of productive efficiency. J Royal Stat Soc 120(3):253–290

Hadad DH, Sugiarto A, Purwanti W, Herman JM, Bambang A (2003) Study regarding the ownership structure bank in Indonesia. Financial System Stability Bureau—Directorate of Banking Research and Regulation of Bank Indonesia (BI-BSSK-DPNP), Bank Indonesia, Jakarta

Hartono E (2009) Analisis efisiensi Biaya Industri Perbankan Indonesia dengan Menggunakan Metode Parametrik Stochastic Frontier Analysis-Studi pada Perbankan yang Terdaftar di Bursa Efek Indonesia, Tesis S-2 Magister Manajemen Pascasarjana, The Economic Faculty of Airlangga University

Iannotta G, Giacomo N, Andrea S (2006) Ownership structure, risk and performance in the European banking industry. In: working paper has presented at a Bacconi University seminar

Jensen M, Meckling W (1976) Theory of the firm: managerial behavior and agency costs, and ownership structure. J Financ Econ 3:305–360

Laurenceson J, Fengming Q (2008) Has minority foreign investment in China's bank improved their cost efficiency? East Asia economic research group discussion paper no. 13, January 2008, School of Economics, University of Queensland, Brisbane. Available at: http://www.uq.edu.au/economics/eaerg/dp/EAERG_DP13.pdf

Mardanugraha E (2005) Banking efficiency in Indonesia learned through parametric cost function approach, Dissertation S3 Economics Study program, the Graduate Program Faculty of Economics, University of Indonesia

Pindyck, RS, Rubinfeld DL (1995) Microeconomic, 3rd edn. Prentice-Hall, China

Rahman NAA, Reja BAF (2015) Ownership structure and bank performance. J Econ Bus Manage 3(5):483–488

Rajput N, Gupta M (2011) Assessing the efficiency of foreign bank in Indian context. Bank Bank Syst 6(2)

Ramli M (2005) Study on efficiency rate of commercial bank in Indonesia and some determinants. Dissertation S3 Management Study program, the Graduate Program Faculty of Economics, University of Indonesia, UI, Jakarta

Rusdi M (2014) Kepemilikan Asing di Perbankan Nasional. http://kinerjabank.com/kepemilikan-asing-di-perbankan-indonesia/

Sans OT, Theng LY, Heng TB (2011) A comparison on efficiency of domestic and foreign bank in Malaysia: a DEA approach. Bus Manage Dyn 1(4):33–49

Al Shaher T, Kasawneh O, Salem R (2011) The major factors that affect banks-performance in middle eastern countries. Journal of Money, Investment and Banking, issued 20 (2011). http://www.eurojournals.com/JMIB.htm

Swai JP, Mbogela CS (2014) Do ownership structures affect bank performance? An empirical inquiry onto Tanzanian Bank industry. ACRN J Fin Risk Perspect 3(2):47–66. ISSN 2305-7394

Wooldrigge JM (2005) Introduction econometrics—a moderns approach, 5th edn. Thompson Learning, USA

Study of Green Banking Practices in the Sri Lankan Context: A Critical Review

P.M.P. Fernando and K.S.D. Fernando

Abstract In Sri Lanka, the banking industry can be considered as a monopolistic competitive market. Therefore, both public and private sector banks are following a range of non-price competitive strategies in order to win the market. In this context, the concept of green banking is becoming a novel technology-oriented strategic initiative for Sri Lankan banks to achieve triple-bottom line business results. Under these circumstances, banks are basically introducing paperless and information technology-oriented banking services to their existing and prospective customers while promoting the bank's role as a responsible corporate citizen toward achieving sustainable development. The core strategy used in this scenario is the use of the term "green banking" as a brand-positioning factor where the above-mentioned set of paperless and information technology-oriented banking services are introduced to its customers. Through this innovation, banks are able to gain cost-effective advantages rather than contributing to environmental sustainability. Therefore, this paper critically reviews the above scenario by using a case-study approach while addressing to the basic question of whether or not the current green-banking initiatives used by the Sri Lankan banking sector are truly contributing to environmental sustainability. The authors explore the above phenomena through a conceptual model and suggest realistic solutions to convert green-banking strategies to achieve long-term sustainable development of both the banking sector and the environment.

Keywords Green banking · Strategic initiative · Branding · Environmental sustainability · Triple-bottom line

P.M.P. Fernando (✉)
Department of Marketing Management, Faculty of Commerce and Management Studies, University of Kelaniya, Colombo, Sri Lanka
e-mail: madhuri@kln.ac.lk

K.S.D. Fernando
XYZ Bank Plc, Colombo, Sri Lanka
e-mail: ksdfernando@yahoo.com

E. Lau et al. (eds.), *Selected Papers from the Asia-Pacific Conference on Economics & Finance (APEF 2016)*, DOI 10.1007/978-981-10-3566-1_10

1 Introduction

Corporations are moving into a new paradigm of corporate governance through sustainable business models that are striving for minimal negative impact on the global and local environment, the community, and the economy. The societal-marketing and the holistic-marketing concepts comprehensively analyze the responsibility of a marketer toward preserving the well-being of the environment and society while achieving its profit objectives. Green marketing or ecological marketing addresses the long-term sustainable achievement of business success while giving emphasis to triple-bottom line profits. Increasing energy consumption and the increase of energy prices, the changes in consumer expectations regarding environmentally friendly businesses, the concerns of stakeholders, including the general public, are among the reasons for an organizations to "go green." In the same vein, green banking is a concept adapted by the worldwide banking industry as a strategic move toward sustainable banking.

A bank is a financial institution licensed as a receiver of deposits. There are two types of banks: commercial or retail banks and investment banks. In most countries, banks are regulated by the national government or central bank. A commercial bank is generally known as a financial institution that provides services such as accepting deposits, providing business and auto loans, mortgage lending, and offering basic investment products such as varying types of savings accounts and certificates of deposit to its customers. The traditional commercial bank is a brick-and-mortar enterprise where front-line staff carry out the traditional teller transactions while providing safe-deposit boxes, vaults, and ATMs. However, modern commercial banks might not have any physical branches and require banking consumers to complete all transactions by telephone or Internet. In exchange, the banks generally pay higher interest rates on investments and deposits and charge lower fees. When focusing on the Sri Lankan scenario, there were 25 licensed commercial banks (LCBs), including 12 branches of foreign banks, and 7 licensed specialised banks (LSBs) by the end 2015 (Central Bank of Sri Lanka 2015).

In Sri Lanka, as a whole, the licensed commercial bank market has a monopolistic competitive nature. Therefore, non-price competition is playing a vital role in gaining market share as well as profitability. In this case, technologically driven product innovations are coming to the scenario as a tool to gain increasing competitive advantages for the firm. The Central Bank of Sri Lanka (2015) mentioned that banks have become heavy adopters of information technology (IT) during the latter part of the twentieth century with the aim of achieving significant improvements in efficiency through automation. The emergence of the Internet and cyber-technologies has enabled the extension of banking services to the customer's doorstep, thus allowing banks to make further gains in operational efficiencies. Clearly there is a tendency to introduce information technology-driven banking products and services as green-banking initiatives in Sri Lanka. This is an organizational effort to re-brand the traditional banking products and services in order to position the concept of "organizational commitment toward environmental sustainability" in the minds of the target market. The expected strategic advantages through green-banking initiatives can be outlined as follows.

- Achieve internal process effectiveness aligned with the balance score card approach
- Achieve long-term cost-effectiveness
- Continuous improvement of quality services
- Build the organizational image as a responsible corporate citizen.

In this paper, the authors critically review green-banking initiatives that are currently being practiced by the local licensed commercial banks in Sri Lanka and their true contribution toward environmental sustainability.

2 Research Objectives

This paper, which follows the case-study approach, identifies the application of the green-banking concept of Sri Lankan bankers. The objectives of this concept paper can be outlined as follows.

- To identify the various initiatives taken toward green banking and environment sustainability by private- and public-sector banks in Sri Lanka.
- To obtain an overview of the extent of application of the concept of green banking within the private- and public-sector banks that are promoting green banking as a strategy in Sri Lanka.
- To critically review the application of green banking by private- and public-sector banks in Sri Lanka.
- To suggest the potential applications of green banking in the context of Sri Lankan banking to achieve better environmental conservation.

3 Research Methodology

This chapter comprehensively reviews the literature on the basis of secondary data collected from various sources including journal and paper articles, research and conference papers, annual reports of banks, official Web sites of banks, newspaper reports, etc. To analyze the green-banking initiatives of Sri Lankan banks, the banks promoting such practices in their corporate promotions are examined using a case-study approach.

4 Literature Review

Green marketing is “a broader concept which incorporates all marketing activities that are developed to stimulate and to sustain consumers’ environmental friendly attitudes and behaviors” (Jain and Kaur 2004). According to Peattie (2001), “ecological” green marketing, “environmental” green marketing, and “sustainable” green marketing are the three phases used to describe the evolution of green marketing. *Ecological green marketing* mainly tries to recognize the products, companies, or industries that directly cause a negative impact on the environment (Yadav and Pathak 2013). In the second phrase, *environmental green marketing*, the focus is shifted to green technology that involves the designing of new innovative products that take into account waste issues and pollution (Azam 2014). Sustainable green marketing addresses green marketing not just in terms of environmental damage and competitive advantage but in terms of the pursuit of sustainability based on futurity, equity, and emphasis on needs, respectively (Yadav and Pathak 2013). A company aiming to be a sustainable green marketer should therefore address ethics, corporate social responsibility (CSR), and the whole environment altogether. Green-marketing efforts can move enterprises to develop “green” brands as well. Chen (2010) suggests that companies should invest more resources in the increasing of green-brand image, green satisfaction, and green trust because all three factors are positively associated with green-brand equity.

The banking industry is the main aid-provider to business development, and they influence the economic growth of a country in terms of quality as well as quantity. Therefore, the role of banks in environmental sustainability is crucial, and modern banks that have identified this causal relationship have taken initiatives to introduce green banking as a practice and a strategy to fulfill their social obligation while differentiate from the rest. Green banking is the operation of banking activities giving special attention on social, ecological, and environmental factors aiming at the conservation of nature and natural resources (Rahman et al. 2013). According to Singh and Singh (2013) “green banking combines operational improvements, technology and changing client habits in banking business while promoting environmental-friendly practices and reducing carbon footprint from banking activities”.

4.1 Reasons for and Benefits of Green Banking

Like any other business enterprise, banks directly interact with the environment through consuming natural resources for their functions and producing carbon emissions. Banks also act as financial intermediaries who are the major source of long-term funding for numerous business organizations that pollute the environment heavily, and thereby the banks also have an indirect influence on the environment (IDRBT 2013). As responsible corporate citizens, business organizations should focus more on safeguarding natural resources and the environment. There is a growing interest as well as awareness among top managers, stakeholders, and academicians on green-marketing strategies and their potential impact on the triple-bottom line (Cronin et al. 2010). Business organizations, including banks, are realizing the importance of the triple-bottom line in their day-to-day banking operations and so their main profit motive has shifted toward achieving a balance between the "three Ps" in achieving long-term profitability. Tara et al. (2015) highlight that banks are fulfilling dual roles that drive them toward the green-banking concept. The first role is to work toward ethically and socially responsible banking; the second is to fulfill their role of corporate social responsibility. This identification is a core factor for bankers to move toward green banking.

Studies are revealing that there is a positive correlation between the environmental performance of a company and their financial performance (Russo and Fouts 1997; Waddock and Graves 1997; Horvathova 2010; Iwata and Okada 2011). Furthermore Russo and Fouts (1997) highlight that with industry growth, the relationship between environmental performance and economic performance also increases. According to Simpson and Kohers (2002), there is a positive relationship between the corporate social performance and financial performance among commercial banks. Corporate social performance consist of three fundamental components: social, environmental, and governance performance (Ioannou and Serafeim 2010). A meta-analysis performed by Orlitzky et al. (2003) comprising 52 studies reveals that corporate virtue in the form of social responsibility and, to a lesser extent, environmental responsibility is likely to pay off in financial performance. The relationship found between the environmental and social performance of a firm and its financial growth can easily lead bankers to implement green banking.

Not only does green banking teach banks to be more productive through better productivity and waste management, the initiatives are also directing these firms to achieve a competitive advantage. Porter and van der Linde (1995) argue that having resources is no longer enough to build a competitive advantage; how these resources are used productively is what makes for competitiveness today. This competitive advantage can be used as a differentiating factor by the bank in their brand positioning as well as social standing. Currently awareness about environmental protection is increasing among consumers. In addition, globalization has increased the spread of information, and stakeholders are more concerned about how each organization is meeting their role of corporate citizenship. Due to this, investors are now opt for environment friendly investments. Orasto (2006) introduced four generic types of competitive environmental strategies (see Fig. 1) in which a classification scheme is introduced that can help managers "optimize the economic return on environmental investments and convert these investments into source of competitive advantage." Banks can use green-banking practices as a point of difference in achieving competitive advantage through the given classification.

Currently there is greater attention from stakeholders on the actions of an enterprise. Not only the direct interacting parties of an organization—such as

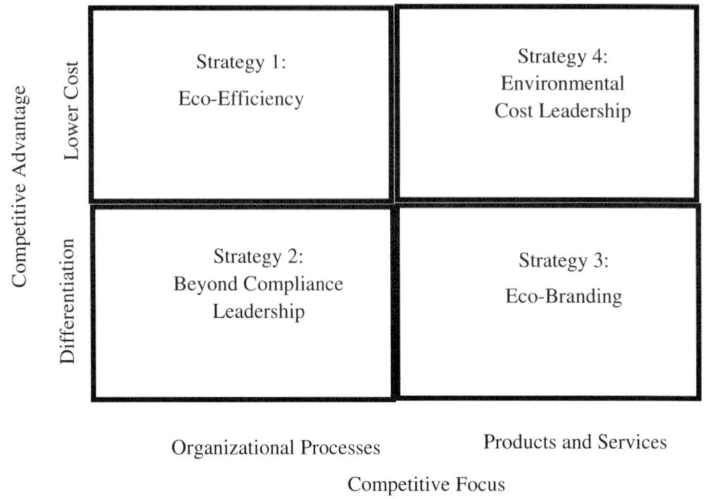

Fig. 1 Generic competitive environmental strategies (reproduced from Orasto 2006)

customers, shareholders, and creditors, etc.—but indirectly interacting parties such as the government and general public also closely monitor the actions of an organization. The perception that environmental labels influence consumer buying decision has increased due to the growing public awareness for safety and preservation of the environment (D'Souza 2004). Green practices among core to non-core banking practices will also benefit organizations to develop a positive brand image and company reputation from a stakeholder point of view. According to Chang and Fong (2010), "green corporate image contributes to green customer satisfaction and green customer loyalty." Choudhury et al. (2013) highlight that banks usually use the term "green banking" along with their prospectus of activities to attract customers to their business organization. They further elaborate that green attitudes and greater environmental awareness among customers increasingly influence banks to carry out environmentally responsible banking activities (Choudhury et al. 2013). At the same time, pressure groups are becoming powerful in the age of digital and social-media communications, and—in the face of that—government agencies are demanding greater disclosure from business organizations. Currently the government is placing stricter regulations regarding environmental preservation.

4.2 *Green-Banking Practices and Products*

Within the common definitions of green banking, the scope of green banking captures a vast range of business functions. The Institute for Development and Research in Banking Technology (IDBRT) (India) report (2013) offers guidelines for greening banking under two levels, i.e., (1) greening banking processes, products, services, and strategies and (2) greening banking infrastructure. These two levels cover introducing environmentally friendly business processes and making information technology and physical infrastructure greener.

In addition, the practices of banks in terms of resource and energy use as well as waste management to decrease carbon emissions are a common practice followed by the banks that are implementing green banking. In addition, investments in green projects, green financing, as well as the use of environmental-impact assessments before lending are also higher-order practices within the green-banking scope. Lalon (2015) points out that there are two ways of green banking practices. One is in-house green banking; another is practiced by bankers in their physical business area. Creating a clean and hygienic banking environment, the development of green buildings, waste management, installation of solar panels on the bank's rooftop, using high-mileage vehicles, decreasing sound pollution, video-conferencing instead of holding physical meetings, adapting online banking activities including online banking statements, and emailing documents: All of these are some of the in-house green banking activities that banks have enacted while financing green projects such as biogas plants, solar/renewable energy plants, bio-fertilizer plants, effluent-treatment plants (ETP), projects having ETP, etc., working on specific green projects, and voluntary green activities, which are major practices by the bankers in their business areas (Lalon 2015).

According to Bahl (2012) and Singhal et al. (2014), green mortgages, green loans, green credit cards, green savings accounts, green funds, green checking accounts, green CDs, green money-market accounts, mobile banking, online banking, and remote deposit (RDC) are among the green-banking products offered by banks. Annadurai (2014), through her study on Indian banks, points out that green-banking technology consists of ATM services, net banking facilities to solar-powered ATMs, paperless banking for customers, clean-energy projects, and even the building of windmills. She further elaborates that introducing as well as promoting mutual funds directed at investments in "green" companies, offering special loan schemes focusing on energy-efficient home improvements targeting homeowners, and introducing credit cards co-branded with environmental charities can also be considered under green-banking initiatives (Annadurai 2014). Bihari and Pandey (2015) point out going online, green checking accounts, green loans for home improvements, green credit cards, mobile banking, using power-saving equipment, and solar and wind energy within the bank fall under green initiatives.

4.3 *Noteworthy Green-Banking Initiatives in an International Context*

Given the greater awareness of triple-bottom line profits, business enterprises around the world are moving into green practices, and a large number of banks and financial institutes are moving into green banking and green financing. The following initiatives are noteworthy among these.

(i) China took a landmark step toward finding a solution for its greenhouse gas emissions through creating new legislations on banking. China's banking and environmental regulators' green credit card policy encourages the banks to decrease their number of loans offered to high-polluting and energy-consuming businesses while lending more to energy-efficient business organizations that focus on the reduction of pollution (IFC 2010).

(ii) Bangladesh Bank, the central bank of Bangladesh, issued a circular on February 2011 on green banking stipulating that banks in Bangladesh were to move through three phrases of green banking practices within the period of 2011–2013 (Bangladesh Bank 2011).

 (a) Phase 1—Banks were to develop green-banking policies and show a general commitment to the environment through their in-house performance.
 (b) Phase 2—Banks were to introduce sector-specific environmental policies, develop green strategic planning, set up green branches, promote an improved in-house environment management, and formulate a bank-specific environmental risk-management plan and guidelines. In addition, rigorous programs to educate clients were to be introduced, and disclosure and reporting of green banking activities were also required.
 (c) Phase 3—Banks were expected to introduce novel products and services and use environmentally friendly actions to address the entire eco-system. In addition banks were to use an internationally accepted format, such as global-reporting initiatives (GRI), to publish independent green annual reports targeting stakeholders.

(iii) The Green Protocol of Brazil, popularly known as Protocol Verde, contains intentions signed by public financial institutions and by the Ministry of the Environment in 1995 and revised in 2008. Protocol Verde is "aimed at defining the initial, multiplying and exemplary banking policies and practices in terms of socio-environmental responsibility and in harmony with sustainable development by public and private banks in Brazil" (Brazilian Development Bank 2011). In 2012, Colombia also introduced a green protocol similar to that of Brazil.

(iv) The Green Funds Scheme in Netherlands is a tax incentive scheme launched in 1995. It comprises with a Green Projects Scheme (which establishes the conditions governing the projects), the Green Institutions Scheme (which regulates the role played by the financial institutions including banks), and, finally, the tax incentive for individual investors (which gets the flow of funds moving) (Ministry of Housing, Spatial Planning and the Environment—Netherlands, n.d.).

(v) The Institute for Development and Research in Banking Technology (IDRBT), which is an arm of Reserve Bank of India, India's central banking institute, introduced a set of guidelines for green funds in 2013, which laid the foundation for Indian banks to look closely at green practices (IDRBT 2013). In addition, they introduced a green-rating system for the banks. However, the successful implementation of guidelines is yet to be monitored.

During the recent past, there exists more evidence on the establishment of separate business entities that are solely focusing on energy conservation, clean and sustainable energy systems, reducing global warming as well as carbon emissions, and overall helping to build a green future. Some of these financial entities are state-sponsored but are closely collaborating with the private sector to increase investments leading to a greener economy. NY Green Bank and Connecticut Green Bank of USA, Green Investment Bank in United Kingdom, Green Fund of Japan, Malaysian Green Technology Corporation, Clean Energy Finance Corporation of Australia, and Green Climate Fund are among these entities. "Green Climate Fund was established by 194 governments to limit or reduce greenhouse gas emissions in developing countries, and to help adapt vulnerable societies to the unavoidable impacts of climate change" (www.greenclimate.fund). In addition, various organizations—including UK Green Investment Bank, Connecticut Green Bank, NY Green Bank, Green Fund in Japan, Malaysian Green Technology Corp., and Clean Energy Finance Corp. (CEFC) in Australia—established a Green Bank Network in late 2015 to increase and accelerate investment in renewable energy and energy efficiency worldwide (North American Wind Power 2015).

5 Green-Banking Practices in the Sri Lankan Context

According to the available literature, it is not a new frontier to provide banking services to the customer by way of technologically adapted delivery channels such as Internet banking or mobile banking. However, within the recent past, the term "Green Banking" became a fancy name across the Sri Lankan banking industry as a brand name for differentiating typical banking products and services. Currently People's Bank, Commercial Bank of Ceylon PLC, and Hatton National Bank PLC are practicing green-banking practices as a business strategy. The authors used eight dimensions—including product types, public announcements, motivation, the concept, services package, the purpose, social-media marketing for green banking, and non-core banking-related green-banking initiatives—to determine to what extent Sri Lankan banks are applying green-banking initiatives. The following one-by-one approach provide the big picture of the nature of green-banking initiatives in People's Bank, Commercial Bank of Ceylon PLC, Hatton National Bank PLC, Pan Asia Banking Corporation PLC, National Development Bank PLC, Bank of Ceylon, and Sampath Bank PLC, all of which are prominent banks in Sri Lanka.

5.1 Green-Banking Initiatives: People's Bank

People's Bank is a fully state owned bank that operates across the country. With >52 years in banking service, it has a network of 347 local branches and 387 service centers island wide. People's Bank introduced Sri Lanka's first green-banking initiative in July 2015. Its green-banking initiatives can be illustrated as follows (Table 1).

5.2 Green Banking Initiatives: Commercial Bank of Ceylon PLC

Commercial Bank of Ceylon PLC is one of the largest private-sector commercial banks in Sri Lanka and is listed on The Colombo Stock Exchange. It has 250 branches island wide and has been rated as the best bank in Sri Lanka by *Global Finance for* the 14th consecutive year. It also introduced green banking in July 2015, and its current green-banking initiatives are as follows (Table 2).

5.3 Green-Banking Initiatives: Hatton National Bank PLC

Hatton National Bank PLC is a private-sector commercial bank operating in Sri Lanka that is listed on the Colombo Stock Exchange. It was established in 1888 and currently has 249 branches spread across the island. It initiated green banking under

Table 1 Green-banking initiatives of People's Bank

Product type	Savings account called "YES"
Public announcements	First ever eco-friendly savings product in Sri Lanka
Motivation	To encourage young people to preserve the environment with minimal use of paper, thereby leading the way for a more sustainable future
The concept	"Go Green with Yes"
Services package	Bank E-statements, debit and credit cards, mobile and Internet banking
The purpose	Green banking as a concept is a proactive and smart way of thinking with a vision to reduce the carbon footprint in the country
Social-media marketing for green banking	Educate the youth on the green concept by providing them with real facts about paperless banking through a Facebook page called "YES"
Non-Core Banking-related Green-Banking Initiatives	Not published

Table 2 Green-banking initiatives of Commercial Bank of Ceylon PLC

Product type	Savings/current/micro-finance credit
Public announcements	Commissioned the first of a new generation of automated cash-deposit terminals
Motivation	To completely eliminate the use of paper, continuing an investment in green technology and sustainable development
The concept	Save the environment with paperless banking
Services package	Green-banking channel: Automated cash deposit, debit and credit cards, mobile and Internet banking, E-Statements, E-Passbook
The purpose	Save trees and help the planet while enjoying even greater convenience than before
Social-media marketing for green banking	Not initiated yet
Non-core banking-related green-banking initiatives	Installation of solar-power systems at four branches

its practices in environmental sustainability and technological innovation in January 2016. The followings can be identified as the bank's current green-banking initiatives (Table 3).

5.4 *Environmental Sustainable Practices of Other Local Banks*

The National Development Bank PLC, Sampath Bank PLC, Pan Asia Banking Corporation PLC, and Bank of Ceylon are also carrying out environmental- and

Table 3 Green-banking initiatives of Hatton National Bank PLC

Product type	Savings accounts, credit cards, current accounts, and NRFC and RFC accounts
Public announcements	Not specified
Motivation	Reinforcing its commitment to environmental sustainability and technological innovation
The concept	"Change Your Address and Win"
Services package	E-statements, ATM, debit and credit cards
The purpose	Reinforcing its commitment to environmental sustainability and technological innovation
Social-media marketing for green banking	Not initiated yet
Non-core banking-related green banking initiatives	Have introduced a few branches that are branded as green branches

sustainability-related banking operations. However, these banks have not yet introduced these practices under green-banking initiatives. National Development Bank PLC recently launched a new personal loan scheme, specially designed to purchase a net-meter solar-power system, for any household. At the same time, Sampath Bank PLC also lunched a credit- and debit-card promotion to their customers to visit and stay at eco-friendly hotels. The purpose of this promotion is also to reduce the carbon footprint to the environment as a result of modern hotel operations. In addition, Sampath Bank PLC has taken initiatives to go "paperless" through relying on e-mediums through e-communications, virtual banking, and cashless transactions. It also encourages green ethics among employees through the environmental pledge they have developed. Apart from that, in 2015, Pan Asia Banking Corporation PLC launched Sri Lanka's first "green" asset-backed securitization with Trillion Investments Limited, which is a licensed investment manager regulated by the Securities and Exchange Commission of Sri Lanka. Bank of Ceylon, a state-owned commercial bank, through their 2014 sustainability report highlighted their contribution of waste-paper recycling, energy conservation, and screening of projects for environmental impact during the credit-evaluation stage.

Apart from these banks, Bank of Ceylon, Nations Trust Bank, Seylan Bank PLC, and DFCC Bank are local banks that carry out projects and provide investments in environmental-preservations activities while promoting renewable energy, waste management, etc.

6 Critical Review of the Application of Green Banking by Sri Lankan Local Banks

In the typical banking-business model, the bank lends money to borrowing parties in the economy. Those parties could be anyone including the range of individuals to corporations to government entities. The main purpose of getting loans from banks is to invest that money into fixed assets or to use it for working-capital requirements. This is the stage at which the borrowing parties are actually using natural resources as an input into their production and consumption processes. However, most of these parties are dumping the negative outcomes back to into the environment as a result of production and consumption.

Figure 2 shows the relationship between borrowing, lending, and how the outcome of core banking activities affect the environment. In a situation like that, banks play an intermediary role and can be the cause of greater environment degradation than the resource consumed through direct banking operations. Banks are calculating the risks of their lending decisions before deciding the investment. Proper risk management is at the heart of a bank's operations, and the success of a bank will significantly depend on these practices. The role of banks in managing environmental risk can be pivotal for a greener economy. According to Jeucken and Bouma (1999), "banks act as assessors of risk and banks are better equipped to

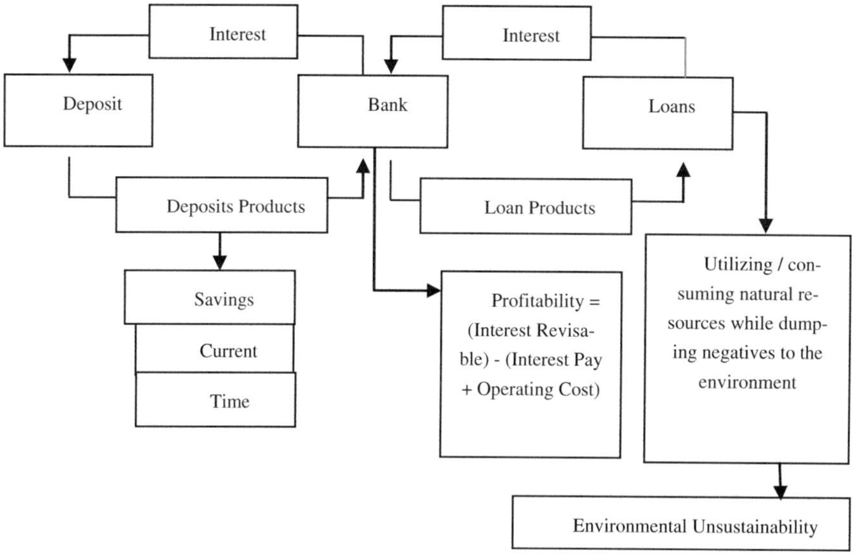

Fig. 2 Banking business and its environmental impact

value the risks of various investments than individual investors who have surpluses available." They point out that banks, by virtue of their larger scale, are more able to spread the risks. If banks do not perform proper risk assessments, negative environment outcomes are inevitable.

The current study revealed the following important factors related to the present Sri Lankan green-banking initiatives.

- Sri Lankan banking enterprises have a long journey ahead in terms of their green-banking strategies. It is a positive factor that most of the local banks in Sri Lanka have introduced green and sustainability concepts into their banking activities. If analyzed from the framework of Peattie (2001), on the evolution of green marketing, Sri Lankan local banks are still either at the stages of "ecological" or "environmental" green marketing. As a preliminary step of reaching the stage of "sustainable" green marketing, the banking system should take into consideration the environmental risk factor of their lending decisions.
- The annual reports of local banks in Sri Lanka are giving emphasis to activities performed under categories of sustainability, environment, and CSR. These activities vary among paperless banking, paper recycling, energy conservations, using renewable energy, educational programs, investments in environmental projects, responsible lending, etc. But whether these are one-off projects or continuous projects is the important question. At the same time, banks are yet to

reveal the exact actions taken on assessing the environmental risk of a credit decision. Proper environmental impact-assessment methodologies have yet be introduced into banking practices and reporting.

- Most of the activities performed by banks in Sri Lanka under the umbrellas of sustainability or the green theme regard in-house banking operations. The key strategy is adopting innovative as well as technologically advanced and services delivery method while reducing paper consumption. Paperless banking processes would enhance the speed of communication flow, energy conservation, and waste management as well as decrease costs to the organization, thus increasing banks' total efficiency, etc. Biswas (2011) states that "adoption of greener banking practices will not only be useful for environment, but also benefit in greater operational efficiencies, a lower vulnerability to manual errors and fraud, and cost reductions in banking activities. Going in the same line, most of these banks are gathering the harvest through better operational efficiency."
- Banks are using the term "green banking" as a key selling point to extend their existing product line. In addition, Sri Lankan local banks are more focused on green-banking activities as a "point of difference" (POD) in marketing communications. The emphasis banks are giving to the green factor in their marketing communication is evidence for the above scenario. Technological transformation of customer-banking processes into online or mobile banking platforms can also be a result due to the globalization process. It contributes to a better environment, but the proportion of customers who are reaping the benefits of such transformation will again determine the total environmental benefit. Green banking should not just be a POD in communication; it should be a POD in banking strategies itself and should embrace a larger proportion of the customer base.
- Local banks are using the term "green-banking practices" as a positioning strategy. According to the study, it is clear that banks are trying to position their image as responsible corporate citizens as well as firms that are paying more attention to environmental sustainability.

In a common platform, Sri Lankan local banking green activities can be summarized in Fig. 3. According to the figure, Sri Lankan local banks are mainly carrying out green banking through the technological transformation of banking services. In terms of market positioning, they are mainly highlighting the bank's contribution toward environmental sustainability as a responsible corporate citizen. This initiative can be identified as a rebranding of the existing product line to increase the value proposition. According to the balance-scorecard perspective, as a whole banks can expect cost-effectiveness in their internal business processes through green-banking initiatives.

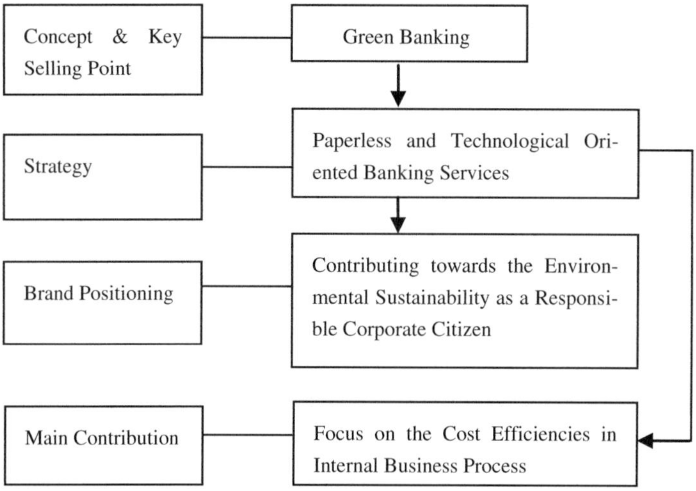

Fig. 3 Green-banking model and environmental sustainability

7 Recommendations

If Sri Lankan local banks truly want to truly position themselves as green banks in par with the best green banks found in the global context, it is imperative for them to recognize their responsibilities as a corporate citizen. Following are some of the strategies to reach the stage of a true green banker.

- International Finance Corporation points out that "97% of the growth in greenhouse gas emissions in the next 20 years will come from developing countries and local banks are playing a critical role in helping the counties to reach a low-carbon future" (IFC 2010). In this context, the banking sector of a country plays a crucial and decisive role in promoting environmentally sustainable and socially responsible investments (Jeucken 2001). "The Equator Principles (EPs) are a credit risk management framework for determining, assessing and managing environmental and social risk in project finance transactions. Currently 83 Equator Principles Financial Institutions (EPFIs) in 36 countries have officially adopted the EP, covering over 70% of international Project Finance debt in emerging markets" (The Equator Principles Association 2011). The Sri Lankan banking sector is yet to become a signatory at this set of environmental and social guidelines on becoming a responsible corporate bodies in a growing economy.
- Environmental-impact assessment (EIA) is a process of evaluating the likely environmental impacts of a proposed project or development in which both beneficial and adverse socio-economic, cultural, and human-health impacts are taken into account. The legal framework for the EIA process in Sri Lanka was laid down in the National Environmental Act (NEA) in 1988. Nath et al. (2014)

highlighted that "environmental management in the banking sector is like risk management because it reduces the credit risk, improves the asset quality and increases the enterprise value." Banks should act as a partner in assessing and evaluating the risk involved before investing in different projects. They should also implement clear procedures in the assessment of environmental risk and environmental audit management, and also they should carry out the assessment of loan follow-up and credit requirement before investing in different projects.

- Banks must introduce new credit and lending guidelines to encourage green lending. At the stage of credit proposal evaluation, banks can evaluate the environmental impact of the project and encourage green projects while discouraging environmentally harmful projects. From higher interest rates for higher environment risk to lower lending rates for environmentally beneficial projects can encourage borrowers to be more socially responsible.
- Currently most of the banks in Sri Lanka have adapted environmentally sustainable technologies in their core banking services. Banks should collectively work toward achieving higher consumer adaptability and transformation of existing and potential customers into these business processes, thus resulting in a cleaner environment.
- Local-bank operations are mainly performed through a vast number of bank branches. Renewable energy use, or just waste management in a few branches, is not going to result in a healthy environment. Banks should focus on adapting the same in-house practices to infrastructure development for entire branches island wide.
- Banks should also focus on selecting environmentally friendly producers and/or suppliers. Examples include using recycled-paper manufacturers and renewable-energy providers. This will increase business opportunities for the sector and encourage investors to invest high in industries that the support environment.
- Banks can reduce their carbon footprint by investing its CSR funds to reforestation, bio-diversity preservation, and environment development projects, etc. This can be identified as a combination of CSR and green banking.
- The green-banking consciousness can usually be high in the higher levels of management because they are the policy makers. Such a consciousness can be decreases with the lower levels of management, and the level of awareness would be least with the front-line employees who serve as the contact point with the bank's customers. For example, Sampath Bank PLC, through their environmental pledge, are trying to change the mind set of employees toward the green concepts. The local banks in Sri Lanka must focus on promoting the available value propositions and benefits of green banking to the employees who are in direct touch with the customers at the front-end operations.
- Banks should show more focus on disclosing and reporting the green-banking activities of the bank. They should focus on past-to-current performance comparisons to indicate their dedication toward a cleaner and greener future, thereby encouraging its stakeholders to be socially responsible.

- Green-banking initiatives should not be limited to brand-image development and brand positioning. It should be an action oriented task to protect the environment as well as work toward sustainable development. In this case, banks should be more innovative to implement or use their CSR fund toward more environmental-protection programs.

8 Conclusion

According to the findings of this study, it can be concluded that Sri Lankan green-banking initiatives are still in the preliminary stage. Most banks are using this concept to improve their corporate image while differentiating their existing banking products in order to compete with their rivals. They should expand the use of environmentally healthy guidelines in their business operations, credit extension, and investment decisions while educating both employees and customers on the benefits of green banking. This endeavor will help banks to proactively improve their environmental performance while crafting long-term values for their business.

References

Annadurai A (2014) Effectiveness of green banking technology of the commercial banks in India. Int J Res Commer Manage 5(12)

Azam M (2014) Green marketing: "eco-friendly approach". Int J Innovative Res Dev. Available via http://www.ijird.com/index.php/ijird/article/viewFile/46783/37944. Accessed 01 May 2016

Bahl S (2012) The role of green banking in sustainable growth. Int J Mark Financ Serv Manage Res 1(2):27–35

Bangladesh Bank (2011) Policy guidelines for green banking. BRPD circular no. 02, Banking Regulation & Policy Department, Bangladesh Bank. Available via https://www.bb.org.bd/mediaroom/circulars/brpd/feb272011brpd02e.pdf. Accessed 10 May 2016

Bihari SC, Pandey B (2015) Green banking in India. J Econ Int Finance 7(1):1–17

Biswas N (2011) Sustainable green banking approach: the need of the hour. Bus Spectr I(1):32–38

Brazilian Development Bank (2011) The BNDES and the green protocol. Available via http://www.bndes.gov.br/SiteBNDES/bndes/bndes_en/Hotsites/Annual_Report_2011/Capitulos/institutional_operations/the_bndes_and_the_green_protocol.html. Accessed 11 May 2016

Central Bank of Sri Lanka (2015) Review on banking sector. Central Bank of Sri Lanka, Colombo

Chang N, Fong C (2010) Green product quality, green corporate image, green customer satisfaction, and green customer loyalty. Afr J Bus Manage 4(13):2836–2844

Chen YS (2010) The drivers of green brand equity: green brand image, green satisfaction, and green trust. J Bus Ethics 93(2):307–319

Choudhury TT, Salim M, Bashir M, Saha P (2013) Influence of stakeholders in developing green banking products in Bangladesh. Res J Finance Account 4(7)

Cronin JJ, Smith JS, Gleim MR, Ramirez E, Martinez JD (2010) Green marketing strategies: an examination of stakeholders and the opportunities they present. J Acad Mark Sci 39(1):158–174

D'Souza C (2004) Ecolabel programmes: a stakeholder (consumer) perspective. Corp Commun Int J 9(3):179–188

Horvathova E (2010) Does environmental performance affect financial performance? a meta-analysis. Ecol Econ 70(1):52–59
Institute of Development and Research in Banking Technology (2013) Green banking. Available via http://www.idrbt.ac.in/publications/Frameworks/Green%20Banking%20Framework%20(2013).pdf. Accessed 01 May 2016
International Finance Corporation (2010) Climate change-filling the financing gap. An IFC report on climate change. The World Bank Group, Washington DC
Ioannou I, Serafeim G (2010) What drives corporate social performance? International evidence from social, environmental and governance scores. Working paper. Harvard Business School. Available via www.hbs.edu/faculty/Publication%20Files/11–016.pdf. Accessed 5 May 2016
Iwata H, Okada K (2011) How does environmental performance affect financial performance? Evidence from Japanese manufacturing firms. Ecol Econ 70(9):1691–1700
Jain SK, Kaur G (2004) Green marketing: an Indian perspective. Decision 31(2):168–209
Jeucken M (2001) Sustainable finance and banking. The finance sector and the future of the planet. Earthscan, London
Jeucken MHA, Bouma JJ (1999) The changing environment of banks. GMI 27 autumn. Available via http://www.sustainability-in-finance.com/gmi-jeucken-bouma.pdf. Accessed 13 May 2016
Lalon RM (2015) Green banking: going green. Int J Econ Finance Manage Sci 3(1):34–42
Ministry of Housing, Spatial Planning and the Environment, Netherland (n.d.) The green funds scheme. http://www.rvo.nl/sites/default/files/bijlagen/SEN040%20DOW%20A4%20Green funds_tcm24–119449.pdf
Nath N, Nayak, Goel A (2014) Green banking practices—a review. IMPACT Int J Res Bus Manage (IMPACT: IJRBM) 2(4):45–62
North American Wind Power (2015) Global green bank network forms to speed shift to clean energy. Available via http://nawindpower.com/global-green-bank-network-forms-to-speed-shift-to-clean-energy. Accessed 14 May 2016
Orasto RJ (2006) Competitive environmental strategies: when does it pay to be green? Calif Manage Rev 48(2):127–143
Orlitzky M, Schmidt FL, Rynes SL (2003) Corporate social and financial performance: a meta-analysis. Organ Stud 24(3):403–441
Peattie K (2001) Towards sustainability: the third age of green marketing. Mark Rev 2(2):129–146
Porter ME, van der Linde C (1995) Green and competitive: ending the stalemate. Harvard Bus Rev 73(5):120–134
Rahman MM, Ahsan MA, Hossain MM, Hoque MR (2013) Green banking prospects in Bangladesh. Asian Bus Rev 2(no. 2, issue 4):59–63
Russo MV, Fouts PA (1997) A resource-based perspective on corporate environmental performance and profitability. Acad Manage J 40(3):534–559
Simpson WG, Kohers T (2002) The link between corporate social and financial performance: evidence from the banking industry. J Bus Ethics 35(2):97–109
Singh H, Singh PB (2013) An effective & resourceful contribution of green banking towards sustainability. Int J Adv Eng Sci Technol. Available via http://www.sestindia.org/wpcontent/uploads/2013/01/Volume-1Number-2PP-41-45.pdf. Accessed 01 May 2016
Singhal K, Singhal K, Arya M (2014) Green banking: an overview. Asian J Multi Stud 2(6)
Tara K, Singh S, Kumar R (2015) Green banking for environmental management: a paradigm shift. Curr World Environ. Available via http://www.cwejournal.org/?p=12902. Accessed 02 May 2016
The Equator Principles Association (2011) Equator principles association members & reporting. Available via www.equator-principles.com/index.php/members-reporting. Accessed 14 May 2016
Waddock SA, Graves SB (1997) The corporate social performance-financial performance link. Strateg Manage J 18(4):303–319
www.greenclimate.fund (n.d.) What is GCF [online]. Available via http://www.greenclimate.fund/home. Accessed 11 May 2016

Yadav R, Pathak GS (2013) Environmental sustainability through green banking: a study on private and public sector banks in India. OIDA Int J Sustain Dev. Available via http://www.ssrn.com/link/OIDA-Intl-Journal-Sustainable-Dev.html. Accessed 01 May 2016

Bibliography

Bank of Ceylon (2014) (2015) Annual report. Available via http://web.boc.lk/index.php?route=information/annualreport. Accessed 15 May 2016

Colombo Gazette (2015) Trillion lead manages Sri Lanka's first 'green' asset backed securitisation. Available via http://colombogazette.com/2015/10/29/trillion-lead-manages-sri-lankas-first-green-asset-backed-securitisation/. Accessed 11 May 2016

Commercial Bank of Ceylon PLC (2014) Annual report. Available via www.combank.lk/newweb/annualreports/CommercialBankAR2014.pdf. Accessed May 16 2016

Hatton National Bank PLC (2014) Annual report. Available via http://www.hnb.net/images/ir/annual_reports/pdf/annual_report2014.pdf. Accessed 13 May 2016

Hatton National Bank PLC, HNB promotes green banking through e-statement campaign. Media Center. http://www.hnb.net/media-center?nid=179

Ideal Green Check, Cheap Solar Solutions in Sri Lanka (2014) http://www.idealgreentech.lk/our-partners/ndb-bank/

People's Bank (2014) (2015) Annual report. Available via http://www.peoplesbank.lk/financial. Accessed 16 May 2016

Sampath Bank PLC (2014) (2015) Annual report. Available via http://www.sampath.lk/en/investor-relations/annual-reports. Accessed 14 May 2016

MIX
Papier aus verantwortungsvollen Quellen
Paper from responsible sources
FSC® C105338

If you have any concerns about our products,
you can contact us on
ProductSafety@springernature.com

In case Publisher is established outside the EU,
the EU authorized representative is:
Springer Nature Customer Service Center GmbH
Europaplatz 3, 69115 Heidelberg, Germany

Printed by Libri Plureos GmbH
in Hamburg, Germany